Steps to Freedom from Lust and Moral Failure

Proven Ways to Overcome Porn and Other Sexual Addictions

By Eduardo Lopez

DORRANCE PUBLISHING CO

EST. 1920

PITTSBURGH, PENNSYLVANIA 15238

Dorrance Publishing Co
585 Alpha Drive
Pittsburgh, PA 15238
Visit our website at *www.dorrancebookstore.com*

ISBN: 979-8-8872-9102-4
eISBN: 979-8-8872-9602-9

Table of Contents

Foreword..1

Sean Dunn describes and validates the struggles faced by someone who battles temptation and the guilt of falling into sin repeatedly. The person desires to be free from destructive habits and seeks God's forgiveness and transformation.

The book, written by Eduardo Lopez, offers guidance and prayers to help individuals find freedom from sexual sin and live a life of purpose and joy in God's love.

Eduardo is an anointed and gifted evangelist with a track record of helping people find hope and healing through his ministry. The book provides a path toward overcoming temptation and embracing God's plan for a fulfilling life.

Dedication..5

Through thick and thin, this unwavering dedication is a heartfelt tribute to my wife, Minnie. It describes her as a source of strength and support, helping me overcome life's challenges.

In difficult times, she has proven to be a trustworthy confidante. The memoir highlights Minnie's passionate love, captivating qualities, and the joy I experience in sharing a lifelong union with her.

The narrative portrays Minnie as a faithful, loving, and delightful partner who has deeply touched my heart since I was seventeen.

Preface..7

Sexual addiction is a sensitive topic having a deep-rooted impact on individuals. I acknowledge the shame and secrecy surrounding the issue, often leading people to believe they cannot escape it.

Also, I offer reassurance that by following godly counsel and yielding to God's Holy Spirit, individuals can experience true freedom from these addictions. Jesus is the source of power and deliverance.

Discover how to overcome lust and immoral addictions with wisdom and insights from God's eternal Word.

Introduction.....................................9

Here, I introduce you to the impact of technology and smartphones on modern society, particularly regarding sexual addiction and immoral behavior. It delves into the widespread prevalence of pornography and sexual temptations, especially among young people.

In this chapter, I highlight the destructive effects of sexual bondage on individuals and relationships, including the pervasiveness of sexual assault and abuse.

It concludes by posing insightful questions about the struggle to overcome lust and the unmatched role of divine power in breaking free from the strongholds of addiction.

A Word of Caution...............................19

Here, I warn you about the dangers of addictions and offer practical tips and wise counsel from God's Word to overcome them. Don't dismiss any advice or think it doesn't apply to you, as that can hinder your journey to total freedom.

The power of sin lies in secrecy, so it's essential, to be honest and take action. Embracing humility and faith will open the door to God's mercy and grace. Let's be doers and overcomers, not just theoretical learners.

May the Lord bless you with wisdom and understanding and empower you to lead others to liberty.

Strongholds....................................21

In this chapter, I delve deep into the human soul to explore how the enemy operates to enslave us. I use the story of Mephibosheth and the real-life example of Susie to illustrate the power of lies and strongholds in our lives.

These strongholds are built on false ideas and beliefs, controlling our thoughts, desires, decisions, and actions. By replacing these lies with God's truth, we can break free from the enemy's grip and experience true freedom.

The key is meditating on God's Word and building our faith shield to resist temptation and deception.

Generational Curses...........................39

In this piece of writing, I discuss the concept of generational sins and how harmful behavior patterns and weaknesses can be passed down through generations. I use real-life examples to illustrate how these issues affect individuals and their families.

I emphasize the importance of recognizing and addressing these patterns, seeking God's forgiveness, and using God's Word for protection and transformation.

I provide practical tips, including personalized versions of biblical verses, to help you overcome sin and temptation and restore your relationship with God and your loved ones.

Personalized Romans Six......................55

In this chapter, I stress the importance of Romans Six as a powerful tool to overcome the lust of the flesh and various sinful habits. I share my experience of initially memorizing the New King James Version of the chapter and finding it challenging to apply.

As a result, I rewrote the chapter in the first person, incorporating different versions to make it more relatable and accessible. I provide you with a personalized version of Romans Six, where you can fill in the blanks with a specific sin or addiction you want to overcome.

The chapter offers practical guidance on memorizing and meditating on God's Word to experience transformation and freedom from sinful inclinations.

Acknowledge the Sins of Your Forefathers...61

I'll introduce you and explore the concept of generational curses and how parents' sins can affect their children and subsequent generations. I emphasize the importance of breaking free from these curses by following God's instructions in His Word.

Instead of blaming and resenting our ancestors, we should confess and repent of their sins, thereby reversing the curse and inviting God's blessings into our lives.

I share a powerful example of reconciliation and forgiveness between a white man and a black mayor, illustrating the transformative power of acknowledging past wrongs and seeking forgiveness. Embracing God's ways and commands brings His favor and grace into our lives.

Dedicate Your Body to God.....................65

Here, I invite you to explore the significance of sincere humility and genuine repentance in unlocking God's mercy and forgiveness. I discuss how the Holy Spirit's work in our lives leads to a rebirth of our spirits at salvation.

I underscore the importance of dedicating our bodies to the Lord as a one-time event, akin to a wedding ceremony, which makes our bodies holy and, thus, belongs to God. Daily, with God's grace, we must yield our bodily members as instruments of righteousness.

I share a sample prayer for dedicating one's body to the Lord and caution against stubbornness and self-will that can hinder spiritual growth and victory over sin. The enemy seeks to outsmart and tempt us, so it is crucial to be vigilant and responsive to God's promptings.

To Disarm Satan in Your Life, Come Clean!...71

This chapter discusses the importance of coming clean and confessing our sins to disarm Satan's hold on our lives. I accentuate that secrecy empowers sin, and God does not bless hidden sins.

Confession and humility before God and others lead to healing and favor from the Lord. I address the deception of Satan in keeping secrets in marriage and the importance of being honest with our children to set them free from the chains of sin.

Ultimately, I encourage you to find freedom through genuine repentance and openness before God and others.

How to Confess...............................77

Consider the importance of coming clean before our spouse, parents, or mature believer. I emphasize that secrecy empowers sin and that true oneness in marriage can only be achieved by removing all secrets.

Well-crated deceptions are the building blocks of strongholds, but confessing our sins and seeking God's forgiveness empowers us to break free. I share examples of individuals who found deliverance through confession and genuine repentance, highlighting the rewards of humility and obedience to God's Word.

Ultimately, I encourage you to seek God's grace to face your fears with a bulldog determination to come clean before your loved ones and find healing and total freedom.

Fear and Love God..................................81

In this chapter, I delve into the idea of being constantly in the presence of God and the importance of walking with Jesus. I highlight prioritizing our relationship with God and having Him as our closest intimate friend.

I discuss the concept of the "secret place" where only God can meet with us and how such encounters can lead to breakthroughs and life-changing experiences.

I share a personal story of facing a crushing defeat, ultimately leading to a more profound love and fear of God. I encourage you to prioritize your relationship with God and seek intimacy with Him above all else.

Have a Battle Plan...................................87

Here, you will learn the importance of being prepared and vigilant in the battle against the lust of the flesh. I compare it to a soldier or athlete going into battle fully equipped.

Satan will try to tempt and allure you, especially when we are out of fellowship with Jesus. To defend against these attacks, I encourage you to walk in the Spirit, meditate on God's Word, and quote key scriptures as your defense.

Visualizing ourselves crucified with Christ can also help us overcome temptation and stay strong in the face of fiery darts from the enemy.

Accountability.....................................91

In this section, I highlight the importance of accountability and fellowship within the body of Christ. We are not meant to be companionless or lone wolves but to be members of one another.

Having someone to hold us accountable fosters spiritual growth and helps us avoid guilt and trouble.

God's restoration and compassion await those who humbly follow His ways, while isolation can lead to despair and spiritual failure, as seen in the story of Elijah. Solomon also emphasizes the value of having a helpmate and confidant to support and lift us up in times of need.

The Four-Second Rule and Journaling......95

Here's a tickle to your imagination: I discuss the fleeting moment of clarity before succumbing to temptation and the importance of developing habits to resist it.

I share the concept of the four-second rule, where I divert my eyes from enticing temptations within a split second. I emphasize the significance of recording blessings and testimonies as a source of encouragement and guidance.

Additionally, I recount a personal experience that taught me the importance of staying vigilant against temptation.

Personal Example....................................99

Learning from the past, I recount my experiences with lust and pornography, starting from a young age. I describe the impact of pornography on young minds and how it continued to haunt me as I grew older.

After becoming a believer, I struggled with the inner battle between my flesh and spirit. I realized the need for God's power to overcome it.

Through attending seminars and studying God's Word, I found freedom from these struggles and now help others in their journey to moral liberty. The steps outlined in this resource can empower anyone seeking deliverance and restoration in their walk with Christ.

Prayer to Recover Your heart and Break the Soul Tie....................................103

In this segment, I explore the concept of soul ties and how they can form with various individuals in our lives, not just romantic relationships. I circle in red the importance of guarding our hearts and the potential damage from emotional attachments to the wrong person.

I share a personal story of a young woman struggling with a soul tie from her past relationship and how she found healing and freedom through prayer and surrendering her heart to Jesus. I provide a sample prayer for breaking soul ties and seeking restoration in Christ.

Praying Out of Temptation Followed by Visualization....................................107

I share insights from Jim Sammons, a businessman and Christian leader who provides tips for memorizing and quoting scripture as self-defense against temptation.

The first tip is to pray for the person or object of temptation, asking God to touch their heart and lead them to repentance.

The second tip is to visualize Jesus on the cross, his body broken, and blood shed for our sins, to remind ourselves of the high price He paid for our redemption and to flee from temptation.

These simple yet powerful practices help us overcome temptation and stay focused on God's truth.

The Rubber Band Technique..................111

Here, you will learn to use physical discipline, such as spanking but with the rubber-band technique, to break negative behavior patterns and develop self-discipline.

I stress the importance of early discipline in childhood and how it helps shape character and behavior. The rubber-band technique can serve as a helpful reminder to stay on guard against temptation and maintain a strong faith in God.

This technique allows individuals to be more alert, enabled, and better equipped to resist the enemy's attacks.

A Loud and Desperate Cry: Abba Father!...115

In this chapter, I discuss the power of crying out to God in total surrender when facing extreme and impossible circumstances.

I share the story of the disciples facing a storm and how they called out to Jesus for help. The chapter brings special attention to the need for unconditional surrender and childlike trust in God's ability to deliver and restore.

I also share a real-life example of a young woman who was released from the shackles of repression and imprisonment by crying out to God in sincere humility and surrender.

The Final Self-Check.........................121

To conclude, you will see the importance of not trying to face struggles and hursts alone. As believers and followers of Christ, we are meant to be part of a community, supporting and re-strengthened by others.

Unresolved past issues can affect our present and future relationships, hindering our ability to experience true freedom and victory.

I encourage self-reflection and facing the truth to break free from the bondage of sin and find strength in God's Holy Spirit, Who empowers us to overcome challenges and experience the fullness of life and love in Christ.

Frequently Asked Questions.................125

As an author, I strive to offer you quick and concise answers to common queries and concerns you may have. By doing so, I aim to save you time and make it easier to grasp the concepts and understand how to approach the issues you are facing. Providing straightforward answers lets you quickly access the information you need to effectively address your challenges.

Facing spiritual battles and the enemy's attacks, asking questions can be a powerful tool. It allows you to gain valuable insights that can guide you in your fight against the fiery darts from the adversary. By addressing these concerns head-on, you can better equip yourself with the knowledge and understanding required to overcome obstacles and find victory in your faith journey.

Moreover, by presenting the answers clearly and succinctly, I aim to empower you to take immediate action and apply the insights to your life. This approach also encourages a deeper engagement with the material and a more profound understanding of how it can be practically implemented in your day-to-day struggles.

Ultimately, I aim to provide you with the tools to tackle your challenges confidently and with a strong foundation in faith. I want to equip you to face and overcome the flaming missiles with resilience and a deeper connection to the author of life, Jesus Christ.

About the Author....................................135

I briefly recount my journey from a troubled youth in El Salvador to finding faith and transformation through Jesus Christ.

After witnessing a classmate's remarkable change, I also turned to Christ and experienced a profound impact on my life.

Through mentorship and studying the Scriptures, I gained wisdom and now help others in their spiritual journey, ultimately becoming a spiritual coach for thousands of people worldwide.

I underline and punctuate the power of God's Word and the rewards of humility and seeking the Lord.

Pay It Forward....................................139

In my final encouragement, I inspire you to become a beacon of hope and liberty for others trapped in sexual perversion. Now you can use your newfound knowledge and faith to help those struggling and lead them to deliverance.

I use the analogy of David and Goliath to convey the power of Jesus in breaking mental and emotional roadblocks and setting the oppressed free. I urge you to be a vessel of God's light and power and use the keys to unlock the chains of those in darkness.

Foreword

You know you are supposed to reject temptation, but you can't seem to break free.

When you stumble, you don't even enjoy it; shame comes rushing in.

You try to pep-talk yourself out of sin, but you keep falling.

You try to strong-arm your way towards purity but still feel dirty.

The memories haunt you...they are so vivid.

The guilt is overwhelming...will it ever go away?

Your promise to yourself to say "no" was real, but you break it often.

You are not who you want to be, so how do you accept God's forgiveness, overcome the temptation, and live as the man or woman of God that you desire to be?

You have heard about "Abundant Life" (John 10:10) and "Freedom" (John 8:36), but you are not experiencing it. Well, there is no better time than the present.

The answers are found in this book.

Eduardo Lopez has done a masterful job of highlighting the problem (both culturally and scripturally), pointing out the consequences, and showing you a path to freedom.

This manuscript is bathed in prayer. Not only were the words written with careful and Godly wisdom, but prayers have been prayed for those who will read it, ingest it, and be transformed from the principles laid out in these pages.

It will take effort... Actually, it will take discipline and hard work, but it is worth it.

Sexual sin is incredibly destructive. It does not create a silo in the heart and life of the slipped and fallen person. Instead, it creates chaos and confusion, and it demolishes everything in its way.

But its reign of tyranny in your life can come to an end.

The bottom line is this: God has a great love for you and a plan for your life. He wants the best for you. He wants you to know freedom from sin, joy in relationships, and protection from an enemy working hard to destroy God's destiny for your life.

He (God) is ready to walk with you to help you overcome habits and reputation. He doesn't just want you to be clean. He wants you to be FREE!

Let me tell you about Eduardo Lopez:

The contents of this book are solid and anointed, but let me tell you about the man who God used to pen these words. Eduardo is a gifted evangelist and faithful servant of our Lord Jesus Christ.

He has served as a volunteer member of our international online ministry team at www.Groundwire.net for over twelve years, and God uses Him in unique ways. For example, recently, he told me that God has used him to introduce almost (I am sure that number has grown since) 1,700 people to Himself.

We do not keep count of the other conversations he has had. Still, I have read hundreds of other chats he has had with people who were lost, hurting, addicted, overcome, or devastated, and with great compassion and skillful wisdom, God has used Him to bring perspective and freedom.

Eduardo is not just a good man. He is an anointed man. He is a gifted man. And he is a man who God uses. So, I am excited to see how He uses this book to impact you and many others.

Sean Dunn
Founder/President
www.groundwire.net

Dedication

To the woman God chose for me to love, cherish, and treasure above all, my dear and precious wife Minnie. From raging oceans to scorching deserts, she's been a tower of strength to face and triumph over life's vexing perplexities.

In woeful and troubling times, there has always been someone I can rely on and trust with the deepest concerns of my heart and the most daunting circumstances.

Minnie is the most passionate lover and partner. As a Juliette, she pulls the Romeo out of me. Her unending charm, captivating eyes, and dazzling smile make our union a lifelong and worthwhile ride.

It's a continuing joy spending my life with the most faithful, loving, and delightful woman who captured and enraptured my heart at seventeen.

Preface

Thank you for taking the courage and time to read this book. The subject at hand is one that most people rather keep private and secret.

For some, it's so shameful and degrading that they believe it will lead to a divorce or career suicide if they admit it.

But worst of all, this weakness of the mind, will, and emotions has a root so deep that it has captured your heart and the most intimate part of your being.

Therefore, some believe it's impossible to break free from it.

The reason is that once you are hooked on porn or other sexual addictions, you don't have the power to overcome them. And if you experience victory, it's only temporary. Sooner or later, you're back into the pigsty.

Let me assure you that if you follow the advice, instructions, and godly counsel, they will prove to you and those around you that God is real and His power out of this world.

Even those deceived into believing that there's no God and that evolution produced something from nothing will benefit from these insights if you yield to God's Holy Spirit.

Jesus has the power to deliver you and wants to set you free. So, let's discover how to overcome lust and the addictions of immorality.

Sincerely from one God set free,
Eduardo Lopez

Introduction

I was born in the early '60s, when color TV made its debut on the world stage. It was the perfect addition to the telephone. Now we had two life-altering devices that opened a window to observe closely and have an ear to the ground beyond borders and across the oceans.

Fast forward to 2008; in forty-six years, technology leaped exponentially to the future, merging those two modern-day wonders into one. Dick Tracy and James Bond's edge was now available to every teenager.

In the meantime, Wall St. and the financial centers worldwide were in chaos. Rich and poor were losing their homes, jobs, and retirement plans. But lo and behold, a genius from Silicon Valley, Steve Jobs, unveiled the iPhone.

A tiny and revolutionary electronic gadget that required more brainpower and a high-tech infrastructure to work than Apollo 11 when it deployed into outer space. It promised and delivered a new way of life and how we experience reality.

Now that you and I have been carrying such a devise and depend on it, here's an essential question for you to ponder and answer "privately" on social media:

What would you be willing to give up so that you are allowed to keep your smartphone?

Would you give up lunch? How about your bed and sleeping on the floor? Would you take a shower every day for the rest of your life?

Don't be surprised or shocked if a young man or woman says, "I would rather have or push for an abortion than lose my phone."

One woman said, "I will walk barefooted for the rest of my life." Another person said, "I will give up sex."

Here's an interesting response from a young man who runs his business from his phone:

"We've already given up our freedom; what else do you want us to give?"

Those are extreme but not uncommon responses.

We use it for communication, GPS, entertainment, also shopping, social media, and millions of work applications. But the sad truth is that besides those conveniences, it has made it easier to lower our moral standards and sin sexually.

It's not uncommon for young, old, male, or female to use online dating, watch pornography, and even self-exposure for fun and profit.

Sexual temptation and arousal in our high schools and universities are as common as hunger pains after a day's hard work. But once they reach out for the forbidden fruit, they get trapped in the lustful passions of the heart.

What's worst is that most students know of someone who experienced sexual assault, especially after drinking at a party.

Many have used a variation of a question on college campuses worldwide. The question is:

Would you sleep with someone for ten thousand dollars? With inflation, that figure is now twenty-five thousand.

Given the right conditions and circumstances, 90 percent of the girls have said yes. The sad but jaw-dropping statistic is that the average is about the same in Christian universities.

The reasoning behind the answer is: "I already do it for free and for fun, but an extra twenty-five thousand dollars will come in handy and will help with my college expenses."

Is it any wonder our "well-connected" generation is dysfunctional regarding wholesome, lifelong commitments and relationships?

Could our young people's minds be polluted with erotic thoughts, ideas, and images?

If that's the case, their hearts are covered in scum, and their consciences are toasted by Satan's flaming arrows.

In other words, sensuality and immorality have taken hold of our young people's lives.

We live in a virtual Sodom and Gomorrah, where millions are hooked on porn and sexual addictions. Their struggles to break loose are like desperately taking a shot at escaping from prison.

After several failed attempts, they give up and believe there's no way out. As we will see later, a breathless voice reinforces the fact they are enslaved and powerless to unshackle from the addiction.

There are many reasons why people fall into immorality, sexual sin, and pornography. For example,

Early exposure to sensual material at home, school, or the internet.
The secret sins of their parents.
Peer pressure to watch pornography or partake in sexual activity.
Responding to temptation's lure and falling for it.
Escaping from reality and the issues of life.
The last one is sexual assault and abuse.

But here's a disturbing fact corrupting the minds of our first-graders. Some perverted schoolteachers encourage kids to find a private place to touch themselves in areas nobody can see.

Their intentions are nothing short of evil. They know it will open the door to a world of lust and immorality. No matter how young they are or how much time has passed.

The instructions will come back to haunt them until they are hooked. The reminder and nagging reinforcement come from demonic forces.

Young men and women have told me over the chat-lines, "I have been masturbating since I started puberty and can't break this habit."

Each of those reasons leads to sexual bondage, developing a stronghold in their souls that will dictate the course of their lives. But like wildfire, it spreads to others in its path, affecting their minds and hearts with intruding thoughts and temptations.

Teenage girls fall for the trap that they must prove themselves through texted nude images to capture a boy's heart. But then, when the boy praises her and asks for more, it's a sign he desires her.

The transition to physical intimacy is only a step away. Typically, it takes place without restriction or little resistance. However, the expectation of loyalty is only a wish that dies down like a candle in the wind.

From then on, hooking up is a game of self-satisfaction to feed their sexual urges. Then, after falling again, feeling down and dirty and empty-hearted, they utter a hollow promise saying that was the last time.

By the time they reach adulthood, oxytocin's God-designed and ordained bonding power becomes ineffective. The numbness of the soul registers no connection. In other words, empty feelings are the new norm.

Just like a Band-Aid, it glues perfectly the first time only. Subsequent uses are devoid of its sticking power and strength. And so, it is with the human heart. But when the ideal life partner appears, it's hard to become one.

Sex is God's wedding gift to bond two hearts and melts them into one integral unit.

Then, He intends it to be enjoyed mutually for the rest of their lives. But to destroy God's plan for our lives, the enemies of our souls work tirelessly to awaken and satisfy our fleshly and sensual desires.

The moment we fall into sexual temptation, we discover it can be the most alluring forbidden fruit. It stirs lustful passions that can enslave us for life. Kingdoms, fortunes, careers, and marriages have been lost for a few minutes of pleasure.

The Scriptures tell us in James 1:14–15:

"But each one is tempted when he is carried away and enticed by his own lust. [15] Then when lust has conceived, it gives birth to sin; and when sin is accomplished, it brings forth death" (NASB).

The rampant and insidious sexual activity in our churches, Christian schools, and universities attests to the fact. It becomes an unquenchable fire and a devourer that consumes our lives when taken to the extreme.

It's an uncontrollable yearning that burns with the desire to fulfill its abnormal and capricious hunger, no matter the cost of the damage to others. The medical community tells us that lust rivals the hold of cocaine.

Consequently, and when inflicted upon others, that traumatic experience produces emotional wounds and scars in their victims that, potentially and if not resolved, will haunt them for the rest of their lives.

It's like an ever-present nightmare embedded in their memory, ready to assault them anytime without any warning. As a result, it's not unusual that the injured party will experience anxiety, insecurity, and unexplained fears.

Yielding to temptation leads to moral failure. Like cancer, it can grow, but it becomes sexual addiction to enslave one for life. Unfortunately, as we will see in the subsequent chapters, it affects the next generation.

One "Christian" man told me his porn addiction led to extramarital relationships with like-minded women. He persuaded his wife to do a threesome. "The first time, she resisted," he said. "But by the third time, she did it willingly," he concluded.

It all started with a secret and harmless entertainment. A moment of relaxation and escape from reality. John reasoned: "When I watch porn, I do it in privacy, causing no harm to others," and so, he deceived himself.

Deep within, like a drug, it began to alter his thought patterns, focusing on filth without regard to decency or morality. As a result, his optical perception rapidly deteriorated into a dark tunnel of false impressions.

It was just a matter of time before the intruding thoughts and temptations reached his wife's heart. Then, unexpectedly, she fell into the trap of guilty but forbidden pleasures.

Perhaps she never imagined it would be her husband, the one dragging her into the shameless cesspool of filth and wild depravity.

That is the goal of Satan and his demons, corrupting and perverting the minds and hearts even of believers.

With such an objective, they destroy the foundation God intended to form through the union of one man and one woman committed for life in holy matrimony. Yet, it's the only pillar that sustains society.

Also, I have chatted with many young men addicted to gay pornography. The hook in their hearts is the same; they cannot pluck it out. "I know it's wrong," they reason. "Because, later, I feel guilty," they conclude.

Conversely, the same happens with young women entertaining lesbian content through sexually explicit internet sites. "I can't stop watching," they tell me. "Only for a short time, but then, I fall again."

The hook is lodged in their hearts as they experience a climax through masturbation. Even though the act is through visual images, it feels natural, as if they were doing it with that person on the video.

After that, no need to watch is necessary. The film plays vividly in the young person's mind. It's permanently burned into the cerebral cortex and deep down the heart and reins. "I call that image to mind with no effort," they confess.

The attacks and urges often come out of nowhere, without warning. Clueless and unaware, the person fails to recognize it's a concerted effort from the depths of hell. "I feel your friend is undressing me," a wife told her husband.

Each time they fall into such temptation, the hold on their souls gets stronger. It's not unlike a swampland. The more they move, the quicker it swallows them up. So many Christians have told me, "I have given up; I can't overcome this habit."

At the same time, oxytocin is released, attaching their hearts to that virtual but surreal person. "I can see her in my mind," they tell me. "And touch her in my imagination," they admit shamefully.

The dominating thoughts, "you are gay," or, "you are lesbian," find their way to the innermost parts of their beings. It wouldn't hurt or matter if the false idea hit them once or twice. But it's a constant and irritating reminder.

Once that is established, the young person believes there is no way out. Therefore, they accept and conclude, "Nothing can change my destiny."

"Why not?" you may ask.

"Because I hear it in my head," they concede in defeat.

However, since the intruding thoughts and temptations come from demonic sources, you know they are false and built on deception. Though overwhelming and overpowering like a lion, they are no match for the mighty hand of God.

But in our world of unenlightenment, Satan and his evil spirits are no respecters of persons or considerate to anyone. So, whether you fool around with straight, gay, or lesbian pornography, his demons are out to enslave your soul.

After many personal battles of triumphs and defeats, the old apostle wrote:

"Stay alert! Watch out for your great enemy, the devil. He prowls around like a roaring lion, looking for someone to devour" (I Peter 5:8 NLT).

So, why can most men and women not shake it off and walk away from lust?

Why do so many repent but can't break free?

Why do so many believe they will die with lust deep-seated in their hearts?

What is the hold in their lives?

2 Corinthians 10:4 gives us the answer to those questions. It reads:

"For the weapons of our warfare are not of the flesh but have divine power to destroy strongholds" (ESV).

Self-examination

Let's pause for a moment and ask ourselves a few questions. The answers will help us deal with the root problem to resolve the initial guilt and, at times, any resentment or bitterness toward that person who hurt us.

How did I discover lust in my life?

____

____

How was I exposed to pornography?

____

____

Did someone induce or pressure me to watch inappropriate images or videos?

____

____

Did someone take advantage or violate me physically?

____

____

Did I take advantage of someone or violate that person physically?

____

____

A word of caution

Not unlike the sign "Danger Ahead," the following paragraphs are written to alert you and give you the tools to overcome any addiction. So, be on the lookout. The war is raging against unseen forces and a formidable opponent that at times seems imaginary.

Again, be forewarned! Within this book, you will find many practical tips, advice, and wise counsel taken from God's Word that have proven effective. They are not opinions or theories concocted in a classroom.

It's easy to listen and dismiss two or three of the points. But, then, rationalize, "They do not apply to me." Half-heartedly, many use the excuse by politely saying, "I don't have a good memory, but I will try." That makes God's Word ineffective and of no use.

I have found that when a person decides an item or tip is not essential, he fails to gain total freedom. It's like someone claiming to be "cautiously optimistic"; his play-dead approach will win the war, right? It doesn't because it's self-deception.

For example, a husband keeps a dirty and embarrassing secret from his wife. He believes the confession will only hurt his marriage. So why start a new fight and ruin the peace at home? "She will never forgive me," he reasons.

He doesn't realize that the power of sin is in its secrecy. Also, as we will see in the subsequent chapters, the enemy's best work is done hiding in the shadows, covered in darkness to enslave our loved ones.

Please, heed the warning. The one thing you might not be willing to do could be the key to irradicating the hold on your soul and setting you free from an invisible enslaver. His craftiness is an odorless venom.

Also, taking action will require a new depth of faith, self-abasement, and humility. That alone opens the fountains of heaven with God's mercy, favor, and grace on your life, family, and purpose on earth.

Listen to the prophet Hanani's wise counsel to foolish king Asa:

"For the eyes of the LORD run to and fro throughout the whole earth, to give strong support to those whose heart is blameless toward him" (2 Chronicles 16:9 ESV).

So, let's begin and wise up! Let's learn how to be a doer and an overcomer, not a "wise" fool basking in the sound of silence reviewing theoretical experience with a headful of useless and soon forgotten knowledge.

The steps to freedom from lust and moral failure are practical and easy, but require sincere humility, genuine repentance, and work. Lastly, if you come with a critical spirit and a closed mind, they will not work for you.

May the Lord bless you with an understating heart to grasp His wisdom.

May He shower you with His grace and favor to be doer of the Word.

And may God fill and empower you with His Holy Spirit to be an overcomer and a faithful witness to touch the lives of many leading them to liberty.

Strongholds

Let's begin to explore and go deep into the human soul to get a grasp of the battlefield and discover how the enemy operates to enslave the hearts of men and women.

In Upwords, Max Lucado asks the following four questions:

"Does one prevailing problem stalk your life?"

"Where does Satan have a hook in you?"

"What is that one weakness, bad habit, rotten attitude?"

"Where does the devil have a stronghold on you?"

What is a stronghold?

A stronghold is a firm and tough-as-nails grip on our souls. As the word implies, it's a clutching strength that dominates our lives.

It can be a common practice, a simple routine, or a family tradition. For example, someone might say, "I cannot eat breakfast without having coffee." Or, "I will not fly on Friday the 13th." Or, "I will not marry someone from the Black Sea." Of course not! There are no islands in the Black Sea.

But the worst are bad habits, addictions, or inclinations that became insatiable desires.

Once we discover and recognize them, we resist them. But, like a magnet, the attraction and enticement keep coming back.

We try to reason them out, but they outtalk us.

They persist and endure through the fight beyond the last round, wearing out our willpower.

Such is a hold on our lives. It lingers on resurging and rising from the ashes to fight another day.

It's like an invisible hand that will not let go. But because it's not physical, like shackles on your feet or handcuffs on your wrists, the victim does not recognize it as such but wonders what keeps him bound.

For the most part, it's the result of a shocking experience or traumatic and damaging event in childhood. Nevertheless, its assault forcefully entrapped our hearts. In time, it distorts how we perceive our environment and reality.

Strongholds are based on false ideas that make sense to our minds.

Therefore, they're accepted. But, in time, they become a conviction leading to a set of wrong conclusions that control a person's life. Last night, Todd told me on the chat lines, "I lost my chance of getting close to God even though I repented."

Once we believe that lie, we act on it, and it becomes a filter through which we make choices. But unfortunately, the mirror is ignored in plain sight, due to the hazing mantle enwrapping it. "God has given up on you, Todd," a breathless voice wisped.

As we develop the habit of seeing our lives through its lens, the grip on our souls strengthens to the point of domination, rendering our wills ineffective. Those false premises repeated over time become our new beliefs.

As we lose our mind's battlefield, our thought patterns get infected with an evil virus. "I've tried everything; nothing works!" "I can't change!" "For the last three years, I've tried to get close to God, but He won't hear me," Todd concluded.

Without our knowledge, Satan and his demons erect a fortress built on persuasive deceptions that support our flawed belief system, one brick at a time. So even after a fervent prayer last night, Todd said, "I hope He heard my prayer."

It's like a cobweb entangling a victim as he tries to escape or as someone trapped in quicksand. The more he moves, the faster he sinks. We do not have the power to set ourselves free. "Did you mean the prayer?" I asked Todd.

"I meant it with all of my heart," he responded.

It takes the grace of God as we humbly seek His favor and deliverance. It's His enabling and sustaining power like eagle wings allowing us to soar despite the pull of gravity.

The Lord has revealed Himself to us as Father, Son, and Holy Spirit. Three persons, yet ONE God. We will never fully understand Him or have a firm grasp of His essence because we are finite and limited individuals.

Even though God is not human, He reflected His image in the most complex creation: man. He endowed us with brainy faculties and some of His awe-inspiring attributes not shared with the animal kingdom.

God created us as spirit, soul, and body.

He made three distinctly different places from which thoughts originate within our bodies, synchronizing with our souls and spirits. They operate in such a flawless harmony that we do not notice it.

In essence, we have three thinking centers. We generate thoughts in our minds in our heads, our hearts' thoughts, and our reins' thoughts, which is called in academia the gut-brain, and we refer to it as a gut feeling.

Science is slowly catching up with the Bible. Even ancient Job foretold some of the most incredible discoveries on the ocean floor and the furthermost galaxies. But our design is the most intricate, captivating, and exciting.

Notice what the Lord says in the following verses:

"I will give my law in their bowels, and I will write it in their heart" (Jeremiah 31:33 DRB).

"Righteousness shall be the girdle of his loins, and faithfulness the girdle of his reins" (Isaiah 11:5 ERV).

The Lord Jesus Christ called out in a loud voice:

"He that believes on me, as the scripture has said, out of his belly shall flow rivers of living water" (John 7:38 AKJV).

The Lord made up the soul in three parts: our mind or intellect, will, and emotions.

The inner man is three-fold: the spirit, heart, and reins.

As we receive the seed of God's Word, it comes through the mind, but then it's planted in our hearts. *"Your word I have treasured and stored in my heart, That I may not sin against You"* (Psalm 119:11 AMP).

Then once firmly memorized and we cultivate it through constant thinking and meditation on it, its roots develop deep down our reins. *"I delight to do thy will, O my God; thy law is within my bowels"* (Psalm 40:8 JB 2000).

Moses wrote: *"You shall love the LORD your God with all your heart, with all your soul, and with all your strength"* (Deuteronomy 6:5). To fulfill God's intended purpose for such command, we cannot but meditate on God's Word.

Out in the meadows under the sun-kissed skies vigilant of his flocks feasting on the greenery, or at nighttide when all is calm and voiceless, David mused pensively: ***"With my whole heart I have sought You"*** (Psalm 119:10).

Let's focus on the soul by picturing in your mind a chessboard. That is the fertile ground where green shoots of wheat begin to grow. But also, the tares appear alongside, making it hard to distinguish them.

Each square is a territory. It's the control center to make decisions. Each move intends to protect, defend, advance, and win like a chess game. But a misstep can open the door to the enemy's attacks, ending in checkmate.

The desires of our hearts dominate the will. It's like the tares growing in the fertile ground of your field, gaining strength each passing day. Or one of your knights fighting without his proper armor. "I should, but I don't feel like it," we might say.

Our deep-seated beliefs in our reins dictate and send orders to our souls through our hearts through neural pathways. Confused, Amy told me through the chat lines, "Part of me is disgusted with my moral behavior, but another forces me, and I want to enjoy it."

Exposing their self-righteousness and hypocrisy, the Lord Jesus Christ revealed telling the crowds: ***"For from the heart come evil thoughts, murder, adultery, all sexual immorality, theft, lying, and slander"*** (Matthew 15:19 NLT).

If we believe a lie, it will control our thoughts, desires, decisions, and actions. Over time, they become the habits that build our characters resulting in our destinies.

I can attempt to change my behavior. However, no lasting result will occur if I don't replace my deep-seated belief system below my heart. ***"I want to do what is good, but I don't. I don't want to do what is wrong, but I do it anyway"*** (Romans 7:19 NLT).

Let's look at an example in the Bible. 2 Samuel 4:4 tells us:

"Jonathan, Saul's son, had a son who was lame in his feet. He was five years old when the news about Saul and Jonathan came from Jezreel, and his nurse took him up and fled. And it happened, as she made haste to flee, that he fell and became lame. His name was Mephibosheth."

Many years later, when Mephibosheth was an adult, King David remembered his covenant with the best friend of his youth, Johnathan, who lost his life in battle. Also, he was King Saul's son, who died shortly after.

For illustration purposes, let me quote from the Message paraphrase as found 2 Samuel 9:1–8.

> ***"One day, David asked, "Is there anyone left of Saul's family? If so, I'd like to show him some kindness in honor of Jonathan."***
>
> ***2 It happened that a servant from Saul's household named Ziba was there. So, they called him into David's presence. The king asked him, "Are you Ziba?"***
>
> ***"Yes, sir," he replied.***

³ The king asked, "Is there anyone left from the family of Saul to whom I can show some godly kindness?"

Ziba told the king, "Yes, there is Jonathan's son, lame in both feet."

⁴ "Where is he?"

"He's living at the home of Makir, son of Ammiel in Lo Debar."

⁵ King David didn't lose a minute. He sent and got him from the home of Makir, son of Ammiel in Lo Debar.

⁶ When Mephibosheth, son of Jonathan (who was the son of Saul), came before David, he bowed deeply, abasing himself, honoring David.

David spoke his name: "Mephibosheth."

"Yes, sir?"

⁷ "Don't be frightened," said David. "I'd like to do something special for you in memory of your father, Jonathan.

To begin with, I'm returning to you all the properties of your grandfather Saul. Furthermore, from now on, you'll take all your meals at my table."

⁸ Shuffling and stammering, not looking him in the eye, Mephibosheth said, "Who am I that you pay attention to a stray dog like me?"

Let's dig carefully and to the bottommost point to unearth some nuggets of truth and discover why this story is relevant to our subject. Also, let's consider how it can be valuable and well-adapted to our daily lives.

When the news hit about Saul and Jonathan's death, it struck fear into the hearts of those at home. They believed David's army would arrive at any moment and kill everyone related to Saul, including women and children.

So, hastily and filled with dread, his nanny ran like a scared rabbit. She took five-year-old Mephibosheth and accidentally dropped him. We don't know the details, but he likely fell from a horse onto a hard surface, injuring his spine.

Without any medical assistance, Mephibosheth remained lame and disabled for the rest of his hard-luck existence. The outlook on his life foreshadowed a bleak and frightening future. Therefore, hiding his misery in a forsaken desert was his only choice.

Verse four tells us he is living in Lo Debar. The literal translation of that place is "without pasture." The practical meaning is Cultural and Spiritual Wasteland, No Word, denoting lack of enlightenment and without a place to feed.

David asked, "Where is he?" The servant responded, "Mephibosheth lives in the middle of nowhere, in a dry, barren, and desolate land." In other words, he is wallowing in his misery, hiding his face in the dust bowl of no man's land.

If it were here in Los Angeles, we would say he moved from the comfort and luxuries of Beverly Hills to the heart and blistering heat of the Mojave Desert. But unfortunately, you can't find his house because there are no roads to it.

Why is he living in seclusion?

Why is Mephibosheth hiding away, detached, and out into exile?

Why would you move to the Mojave Desert?

Why do you grope like an outcast?

One word, fear! If you had the opportunity to interview Mephibosheth and ask those questions, he would respond: "Just like my grandpa Saul was hunting down David to kill him, now he will do the same thing to me, right?"

The name Mephibosheth means the end of shame, or Shame No More. So, what kind of lies do you think the devil fed Mephibosheth all these years? What did he believe that caused the young man to disappear off the face of the earth?

Undoubtedly, as nightfall approached, instead of basking in the day's accomplishments and achievements, that familiar and cruel voice returned with evil thoughts like:

Look at you, what a shame, the only heir to Saul's throne, lame, crippled, and handicap.

You cannot even stand on your two feet.

When David finds you, he will finish you like a dead dog.

So, hide in this forsaken place just like you are repudiated, abandoned, and full of shame.

Unexpectedly, King David summons Mephibosheth to appear. He cannot hide anymore. Saul's enemy has finally found him. In silence, he muses, "The dreaded day of reckoning is here, and I feel caught like a rat in a trap."

Verses 6–7 read:

"When Mephibosheth, son of Jonathan (who was the son of Saul), came before David, he bowed deeply, abasing himself, honoring David.
David spoke his name: "Mephibosheth."

"Yes, sir?"

7 "Don't be frightened," said David. "I'd like to do something special for you in memory of your father, Jonathan.

To begin with, I'm returning to you all the properties of your grandfather Saul. Furthermore, from now on, you'll take all your meals at my table."

What a grand and extraordinaire red-carpet reception! Instead of facing execution, the obscure and inglorious heir of a fallen king, now, for the rest of his life, he will dine sumptuously alongside the reigning monarch.

Suddenly, Mephibosheth is rich beyond his wildest dreams! But is that what he expected? Does he believe the enthroned King David will make good on his word? Is this a sophisticated mousetrap? Let's look at his response in verse 8:

"Shuffling and stammering, not looking him in the eye, Mephibosheth said, "Who am I that you pay attention to a stray dog like me?"

The NKJ reads: *"What is your servant, that you should look upon such a dead dog as I?"*

The CEV reads: *"Why should you care about me? I'm worth no more than a dead dog."*

Do you think this young man lived a comfortable, low-keyed, and peaceful lifestyle without the worries of daily life? Or was he in seclusion, fearful, and hiding from his grandpa's vengeful enemy in the worst place on earth?

Such is Satan and his host of demons' cruel and heartless undertaking. Their lies and deceptions can keep you hostage and paralyzed for life! That was Mephibosheth's case. Any one of us in his shoes would feel chicken-hearted.

But fortunately for Mephibosheth, King David didn't follow the customary and popular traditions. Instead, the monarch made good on his word and blessed the young man abundantly for the rest of his life. The truth set Mephibosheth free!

Let me illustrate it with an example. Not long ago, a depressed and suicidal young woman came through our online ministry asking for help. I will call her Susie. However, most people who chat with us use a pseudonym to keep their identity secret.

As I chatted with Susie, she revealed her addiction to lust and masturbation. The degenerative habit kept the teenage girl doing it several times, day and night, every day. It seemed as if an unseen hand dominated her will as if by magic.

In her plea for help, Susie told me: "Nothing works! I read the Bible and pray and cannot get rid of this addiction. Even though I have been under the care of a psychiatrist, nothing helps." She was sick and tired of her vain attempts.

So, in a long chat conversation, I asked, "Did anyone hurt you in the past, Susie?"

"Yes," she responded. "I was raped."

"I'm so sorry, Susie. I'm sorry someone with such evil intentions assaulted, violated, and took your innocence," I responded.

"Did you blame God for not protecting you?" I asked.

"Yeah, I am bitter against God," she continued.

"Did you conclude that since God did not preserve your innocence, what's the point of staying pure?"

"Yes," she typed in the chat box.

"So, you gave in to immorality," I asserted.

"Yes," Susie concluded. From a victimized child and wounded soul's point of view, Susie told me how she perceived her messed-up and painful world now.

Those arguments wouldn't have made sense if the assault had not happened. But now, "What's the worst that can happen to me? That man took my innocence by ravishing my body. I'm not pure anymore but dirty." And so, Susie reasoned.

I led her in the steps to freedom from lust and immorality with the tips in this book. Also, God delivered her from the stronghold of bitterness after she forgave her perpetrator. I gave Susie the tools to use offensively against temptation.

The Holy Spirit used His Word and wisdom to cleanse her heart and replace the lies Satan fed Susie after the assault. But, unfortunately, with reinforcement, some deceptions are seated deeply in the innermost chambers of the heart and reins.

Some of the lies were,

"Now you are worthless,"

"You are dirty,"

and "You will never be pure again."

But as typically happens, the internal pain was so severe and at times unbearable.

Therefore, Satan and his demons offer a solution. They encourage and persuade their victims with a systematic list of quick fixes to numb the pain but strengthen their grip on their souls. But unfortunately, the schemes work.

"Replace the pain with sex, masturbation,

go ahead and take a drink,

and cut yourself.

It will mitigate the pain."

What the enemy was doing was leading this girl in a series of steps to destroy her life. Like a lamb to the slaughter, Susie was slowly descending into a path dark as a dungeon. Medication relieved her downheartedness but only temporarily.

And when nothing alleviates the stress, heartaches, bitterness, anxiety, and depression, there is the ultimate solution. Can you guess what that is? Yes, suicide. "I'm falling apart and to pieces. I'm emotionally shattered. I have no reason to live."

That is sad and, unfortunately, common. We chat with the Susies of this broken world every day. In their minds, they reason and ask, "That will stop the pain, relieve the stress, cure the depression, and put an end to my misery, right?"

That is how the Evil One and his host of wicked but unseen ghouls skillfully use lies and deceptions to build strongholds within the souls of their victims. Ephesians 4:27 in the Amplified Bible reads:

"Nor give place to the devil." Or, "Leave no [such] room or foothold for the devil [give no opportunity to him]."

The original Greek word translated "place" is ***topon***, which comes from ***topos***, where we derive the term topography. Therefore, it refers to a literal ground. It's not a symbolic expression but a precise location or territory.

That chessboard I referred to initially is the ground Satan wants to control to manipulate your life. At the same time, God wants to build towers of truth. You decide who you will believe and allow to encamp, set down roots, and finally reside in your soul.

Back to Susie's story.

After God set her free, the towers of truth replaced the strongholds of lies on the battlefield of Susie's soul. When God's Holy Spirit uproots the hotbeds of dark and crooked ways, He gives you a clean and smooth slate.

Susie was ready to erect a fortress based on God's Word. So, I taught her: The next time the devil hurls a flaming missile to make you fall, visualize in your mind, and see yourself on the cross with Jesus and say:

"I have been crucified with Christ, and I no longer live, but Christ lives in me. The life I now live in the body, I live by faith in the Son of God, who loved me and gave himself for me" (Galatians 2:20 NIV).

God's holy and uplifting thoughts replaced the insidious and demonic schemes. So then, God's towers of truth replaced the devil's strongholds. Don't underestimate those evil spirits. They come back strong, but now you are not alone nor defenseless.

I kept in touch with this young woman. That Sunday, after our online conversation, Susie reduced the masturbation from twenty to three times. That was a significant improvement. But the next day to only one. After that, to zero. So, God gave her the victory against temptation.

One week later, and by email, Susie told me, "I have made the Scriptures my own. It's been a whole week that I have not fallen into temptation," she reported happily. Susie is protected as long as she keeps the shield of faith in place.

Concluding her remarks, Susie wrote: "For the first time, I have experienced total freedom. I am not a slave anymore." That sounds odd or irrational to some, but it's heartfelt, like your mother's voice when lost in the woods at nightfall.

Such is the power of God's Word! Of course, you can't change your behavior, but if you replace Satan's thoughts with the thoughts of God, the transformation will happen. Each verse you memorize and meditate on builds your shield of faith.

Self-examination

Let's pause for a moment and review the questions in this chapter. The purpose is to discover and identify any strongholds in your life.

Is there a common practice, routine, or tradition you follow but now you question why you do it?

____

____

Is there a life issue you constantly deal with but wish it would disappear? (it could be making a wrong choice or an improper attraction).

____

____

Is there a bad habit you wish to conquer?

____

____

Is there a weakness that controls your life?

____

____

What is the hold on your life that overpowers your will?

____

____

Generational Curses

In her book, ***Milk and Honey***, Rupi Kaur writes:

"You look just like your mother.
I guess I do carry her tenderness well.
You both have the same eyes.
Cause we are both exhausted.
And the hands.
We share the same wilting fingers.
But that rage, your mother doesn't wear that rage.
You're right. This rage is the one thing I get from my father."

I wouldn't doubt Rupi can make the connection to grandparents also. Even in the third and fourth generations, the innate tendencies and inclinations to sin in a particular area pass down to children. But that seed does not die; a new descendant inherits it.

Often, when a father or mother's life is manipulated by a stronghold, involuntarily, they are teaching their child the same behavioral patterns and weaknesses of the soul. What they see and perceive in us; they embrace and carry on.

Just like we inherit physical features from our ancestors, we also get the root problems. Those issues can be genetically transmitted or taught by conduct and demeanor. "You are just like your mother" is an insult but many times undeniable.

Let me illustrate with a true-to-life example. I heard the sad story of a woman who suffered the tragic ending of her first marriage and child. Her course of events followed a long life of hardships and spousal abuse from her second husband.

Without knowing Jesus or having the counsel of a godly mentor, Mary succumbed to the feelings of her heart, and her life spiraled downward. Slowly, a deep root of bitterness developed and grew to control her days.

As her children grew up, they struggled with the same root problems and fears. Even though they did not suffer as much as Mary did, forgiving an offender is still a complex issue and a sealed book for them today.

The Scriptures tell us,

"Do not bow in worship to them, and do not serve them; for I, the LORD your God, am a jealous God, bringing the consequences of the fathers' iniquity on the children to the third and fourth generations of those who hate me, but showing faithful love to a thousand generations of those who love me and keep my commands" (Exodus 20:5–6 CSB).

Let's read about another rawboned and heart-wrenching story that I keep in my prayers. As I was working the chat lines, a twenty-one-year-old woman from India came through asking for prayer. I will call her Nisha. Here's how the conversation went.

"I need prayer," she typed.

"Sure, what's your prayer request?" I responded.

"My mother is a prostitute," Nisha countered. "I am her only child, and she raised me to become just like her."

"Why don't you leave?" I asked.

"I cannot just walk away and abandon my mom," she responded, concerned about her mother. "If I leave, she will not survive. I am her source of income. Now, her clients come for me, not for her, because she is older."

"So, you are her slave," I continued.

"Yes, I am, and I hate this lifestyle. I want to be set free from this bondage and live a regular everyday life," she pleaded to ask for prayer.

At that moment, her mother interrupted, "Get ready to serve a walk-in client, Nisha," she said.

In the seminar on Basic Youth Conflicts, I learned from Dr. Bill Gothard seven non-optional biblical principles. Among them, it's the maxim of authority. In that lesson, he illustrates how God set an umbrella of protection for those under our care.

At home, it is mom and dad, particularly the father. The man of the house is the leader and protector of his family. To get to his children, an intruder must overpower him. Then, it's easy to enslave them, including his wife.

Unfortunately for Nisha, she has no father, and her mother has been an enslaved call girl in that horrible industry since her youth. Being blindfolded spiritually and trapped physically, the woman saw no other option for her daughter's future.

Here's how Jesus simplified it for the attending crowds:

*"**Who is powerful enough to enter the house of a strong man and plunder his goods? Only someone even stronger—someone who could tie him up and then plunder his house**"* (Mark 3:27 NLT).

In the physical as well as the spiritual world, the same concept applies. All a thief needs is a small crack in the back window. It can happen to the adjoining property owner's house as well as your neighbor's mind, will, and emotions.

Satan and his demons work diligently to create a small opening in the soul of a father. Like a dangling shiny object, it captures his attention without seeing the hand that pulls the string. Before he knows it, the beguilement has started.

Those breathless voices whisper thoughts and ideas to tempt a man. For example, check out this new website, talk to that new coworker, or click on that link. There's a sense of urgency to capture that exciting and promising moment.

That ingenious man has no idea the bait has a concealed hook. Once he bites, the bondage starts. The more he engages in immoral thoughts leading to virtual or physical activities, the less he can protect his family.

Each failure creates an ever-growing hole in his covering umbrella, getting his wife and children wet. Of course, he might still be unsuspecting and clueless. However, lacking adequate protection, his family is now vulnerable to the enemy's attacks.

It sounds farfetched and illogical, but the stories abound, following the same pattern and structure. Like in the case of the young Indian woman, her mother lives in a lifelong cage. Her vision or lack thereof is a blurred and obscure delusion.

Let's go behind the scenes and observe how the enemy's tentacles reach our loved ones and begin working havoc upon their lives. Notice how the demonic strategies are insidiously crafty and skillfully carried out.

An unsuspecting wife wonders why she has impure thoughts and dreams.

The children are having sexual temptations never experienced before.

Predators seem to appear from nowhere, making advances.

Once they yield to temptation or suffer humiliation, they receive new instructions:

"Don't tell anyone, especially your dad. He will be ashamed of you."

Here's what fathers who have understood this concept and decided to confess to their wives and children discovered. First, they have been blown away by the damage occurring in the hearts of their loved ones.

They swore on their mother's grave that their sinful and immoral activities were 100 percent secretive. "When I watch pornography, I don't hurt anyone," they believe. "My wife and children won't be affected because what they don't know can't hurt them."

They had no idea their wives, sons, and daughters were struggling with attacks from the enemy in the same area of defeat. But conversely, it also happens when the roles are in reverse. If the wife is sinning secretly, her family is at risk.

The assaults range from intruding thoughts to temptations, unexplained anxiety, depression, physical advances, and even predatory dangers. "I thought of having an affair. Then out of nowhere, this man smiled at me. I couldn't believe it!"

Molested boys carry the humiliation and stigma they are different. "How come you always sit by yourself?" other kids at school ask.

"If I try to make friends, they will know I am weird," they ponder in their hearts.

"If you tell your dad," an inaudible voice in their minds warns them, "he will be ashamed of you and think you are a disgrace." But then, the stranger will whisper and persuade him, "You are the target because you are gay."

Such was the disturbing truth a father learned after asking his wife and children if they had experienced any unusual immoral thought, temptation, attack, or dream. When they revealed their inner but strange struggles, he was blown away!

The good news is that when we come in sincere humility before God, our spouses, and children, the Lord gives us His favor and forgiving grace in the eyes of our loved ones.

In essence, the curse becomes of no ill effect and powerless. Then, we have the opportunity to restore and breathe new life into our relationships. The lies of the enemy dissipate like a morning fog. It is only then that we can fully protect our families.

Jesus taught,

"A good man out of the good treasure of his heart brings forth good, and an evil man out of the evil treasure of his heart brings forth evil" (Luke 6:45).

Any loving wife, adoring son or daughter will follow and submit to a humble, repentant, and broken man's leading. What moves their hearts to respond in such a way is God's grace and favor. They see it in his eyes and discern it in their spirits.

No matter how low he falls, the blood of Jesus is sufficient and will cleanse him and his family from any generational curse and bring about God's grace and favor on their lives. The old prophet wrote,

"I will bless those who have humble and contrite hearts, who tremble at my word" (Isaiah 66:2 NLT).

Let's review the simple method from God's Word that really works!

James 1:14–15 says:

"But each one is tempted when he is carried away and enticed by his own lust. 15 Then when lust has conceived, it gives birth to sin; and when sin is accomplished, it brings forth death" (NASB).

And Ephesians 4:27 tells us:

"Nor give place to the devil." Or "Leave no [such] room or foothold for the devil [give no opportunity to him]" (AMP).

Based on these verses, let me explain a concept and listen carefully to their application.

You and I have a weakness and a particular inclination to sin without exception. So, having that insight, our enemy will persist and capitalize on it.

However, Satan does not know it, so he will tempt you until he discovers that weakness.

Also, that demonic voice will whisper thoughts and ideas to lead you in that direction. But unfortunately, most people never figure out the source of such reflections. It's an intrusion that goes undetected.

In his pursuit, the devil lures you with attractive bait. There is a concealed hook in it. Once you bite, you are trapped! No matter what you do, you can't get rid of it. You don't have the power to liberate yourself.

Such is the feeling of a young man who views pornography for the first time. He is shocked to the core and eclipsed by the shameless and depraved images.

Like a shadow, they will follow by day. But by night, those lewd pictures become not unlike a predator assaulting the young man's mind and heart.

Even though the experience is wicked and corrupt, it awakens a natural desire God intended for a mate to fulfill once married. But the best way to enslave him is to meet that need prematurely and in the wrong way.

The dopamine rush will cause him to crave more to repeat that satisfying but thrilling experience. Each time he yields to temptation, the addiction gains strength and control over the individual's will and emotions.

There are hope and a solution. Let me show you how God can set you free and remove the hook from your soul.

Because you gave the devil an opportunity and surrendered ground to him by taking his enrapturing bait, you need a higher power to recover it. However, you do not have that power; only God does!

Make sense?

Here's a second illustration to clarify the method Satan and his demons use:

Picture in your mind a bull with a ring pierced in its nose. No matter how strong the beast is, its master can easily dominate him by pulling the ring.

You are the bull, and you are powerless to remove the ring.

In reality, what happened is that you allowed the enemy to build a stronghold, a fortress in that ground, as described in 2 Corinthians 10:4. It reads:

"For the weapons of our warfare are not of the flesh but have divine power to destroy strongholds" (ESV).

To start the recovery process, here are the steps you MUST follow:

Of course, the first thing you must do is to repent.

That is, to recognize before God you sinned and are willing to humble yourself before Him, asking for mercy and forgiveness.

Then, in prayer, you must ask the Lord to cleanse you with the blood of Jesus and take back the ground you yielded to Satan.

After the Lord sets you free, you will learn to use God's Word effectively. It's the memorization and meditation (M & M) that keeps the U-turn moving forward and away from the lures and traps of Satan.

Here's a sample prayer to follow. You MUST tell the Lord these words WHOLEHEARTEDLY. It's not a mantra or mental exercise. Don't recite it to God like a poem expecting any fruit in your mind, will, or emotions.

Also, DO NOT let your debased mind rationalize if this activity should work or if it has any merit. Undiscerning, Simple Simon cast the "stone" found in the oyster's mouth into the sea.

(NOTE: If you have not had the experience of being born again, this book can't help you. However, if you want God's favor on your life, use the following prayer to turn your life over to Jesus Christ, repenting your sins and surrendering your entire being to Him.)

To prevent frustration and the sting of failure, you MUST do it with a loud voice and, again, mean the words with all your heart. So, get alone with God and take a giant step of faith. Here it is:

Dear Father in heaven,
I come to you in the name of your only Son, Jesus Christ.
Father, I sincerely repent for sinning against YOU with my lustful behavior.
I yielded ground to the devil by falling for his temptations, and I am genuinely sorry.
Father, forgive me and restore my soul.
Please, Lord, restore my mind, my will, and my emotions.
With the blood of Jesus, cleanse me of all my sins.
Yes, Lord, cleanse my heart of my iniquity and make me whole again.
Restore my fellowship with YOU, Oh God.
Fill me with your Spirit,
So that your Spirit will lead me in the path of righteousness.
So that your Spirit will teach me to walk in your ways.
So that your Spirit will instruct me in your wisdom, and I can learn to make the right choices.

So that your Spirit will rebuke me when I go astray.

And so that your Spirit will comfort me.

Give me your grace,

So that I will have the desire and the power to obey you,

And so that I will be enabled to do your will in the power of your Spirit.

Give me your word,

So that I will have the Sword of the Spirit and learn to use it to defend myself.

And so that I will have the mind of Christ and think your thoughts.

And now Father,

I ask You to take back the ground I yielded to Satan and set me free.

Only YOU, Oh Lord, have the power to destroy the strongholds of the devil.

Replace them with your powerful towers of truth.

For I pray in the mighty name of Jesus, amen!

Assuming you meant the prayer, let's learn how to effectively use the Sword of the Spirit to protect and defend yourself!

Galatians 2:20 says:

"I have been crucified with Christ, and I no longer live, but Christ lives in me. The life I now live in the body, I live by faith in the Son of God, who loved me and gave himself for me" (NIV).

You MUST memorize and meditate on this verse. Without such initial but vital commitment, there will not be any other defensive protection against the enemy's flaming missiles hurling at you.

They are designed to ignite your heart's burning passions of lust, whether in an awe-striking picture or a film or person. The attacks come unexpectedly, disguised like lovesick puppies, but their fangs drip venom like honey.

King Solomon paints a vivid picture depicting the interaction between an attractive woman and a simple but naïve young man. Next, let's read Eugene H. Peterson's paraphrased rendering of Proverbs chapter seven.

1-5 Dear friend, do what I tell you; treasure my careful instructions. Do what I say, and you'll live well. My teaching is as precious as your eyesight— guard it!

Write it out on the back of your hands; etch it on the chambers of your heart. Talk to Wisdom as to a sister. Treat Insight as your companion. They'll be with you to fend off the Temptress—that smooth-talking, honey-tongued Seductress.

6-12 As I stood at the window of my house looking out through the shutters, watching the mindless crowd stroll by, I spotted a young man without any sense arriving at the corner of the street where she lived, then turning up the path to her house.

It was dusk, the evening coming on, the darkness

thickening into night. Just then, a woman met him—she'd been lying in wait for him, dressed to seduce him.

Brazen and brash she was, restless and roaming, never at home, walking the streets, loitering in the mall, hanging out at every corner in town.

13-20 She threw her arms around him and kissed him, boldly took his arm, and said, "I've got all the makings for a feast—today I made my offerings, my vows are all paid,

So now I've come to find you, hoping to catch sight of your face—and here you are! I've spread fresh, clean sheets on my bed, colorful imported linens. My bed is aromatic with spices and exotic fragrances.

Come, let's make love all night, spend the night in ecstatic lovemaking! My husband's not home; he's away on business, and he won't be back for a month."

21-23 Soon she has him eating out of her hand, bewitched by her honeyed speech.

Before you know it, he's trotting behind her, like a calf led to the butcher shop, like a stag lured into ambush and then shot with an arrow, like a bird flying into a net not knowing that its flying life is over.

24-27 So, friends, listen to me, take these words of mine most seriously. Don't fool around with a woman like that; don't even stroll through her neighborhood.

Countless victims come under her spell; she's the death of many a poor man. She runs a halfway house to hell, fits you out with a shroud and a coffin" (MSG)

Once again, here's our first verse in our line of defense.

Galatians 2:20 says:

"I have been crucified with Christ, and I no longer live, but Christ lives in me. The life I now live in the body, I live by faith in the Son of God, who loved me and gave himself for me" (NIV).

Here are a few practical and effective tips on how to chew and meditate on God's Word:

In your mind, picture yourself on the cross crucified with Jesus. (Not that you deserve it or to feel the pain, but to consider yourself dead to sin. See Romans 6:11 below.)

Do it each time the devil comes back with a new temptation to make you fall.

So, when you have a flashback of a dirty memory or picture, you MUST quote this verse from memory and VISUALIZE yourself on the cross with Jesus!

Now, you are on a leveled playing field, and you have the most dominant defensive weapon against temptation. Satan and his demons have no power or authority against God's Word when you personalize it.

Memorization and meditation on God's Word are the two essential activities that build our shield of faith (M & M).

The result is multifold and diverse, affecting many areas of our lives. For example,

    having victory over sin and temptation.

    success in our calling.

    wisdom to make decisions.

    insights, understanding, and influence to help others.

Again, quote Galatians 2:20 from memory in the first person coming from your heart, believing you have died with Christ to your old self and sinful nature. Then, visualize yourself alive and victorious with Jesus in your new spiritual birth.

One chapter within God's Word is designed to quench the flaming missiles hurled at you and overcome the guiles of temptation and its resulting entrapping sin. It's not The Antidote but a significant piece of the puzzle.

Other fundamental and essential aspects like confession and being under proper authority make the Christian life upright and flourishing. Nevertheless, it feels thorny and ill-timed to do. Sometimes, it doesn't make sense. However, God delights to reward it.

The most crucial chapter in the Bible to overcome the lust of the flesh is Romans Six. This chapter has the power to overcome any carnal inclination, sinful habit, or sexual addiction if you memorize it and meditate on it.

Initially, I memorized the New King James Version. However, it was difficult for me to apply it. Therefore, I re-wrote it in the first person and composed it from different versions to make it easier to use. The result has been compelling.

All you must do is fill in the blank about what sin or addiction you want to overcome.

Here's the entire text, and below it, it's the link to the one-page document:

Personalized Romans Six

1. What shall I say then? Shall I continue in the sin of _____ that grace may abound for me?

2. God forbid! How shall I that am dead to the sin of _____ live any longer therein?

3. Don't I know that when I was baptized into Jesus Christ I was baptized into his death?

4. Therefore I am buried with Him by baptism into death that like as Christ was raised up from the dead by the glory of the Father; even so I also should walk in newness of life.

5. For if I have been united with Him in the likeness of his death, I shall also be united with Him in the likeness of his resurrection.

6. Knowing this that my old man was crucified with HIM in order that sin's dominion over my body may be destroyed (abolished) and henceforth I should not serve sin.

7. Being dead, I have been set free and delivered from the power of sin.

8. Now that I have died with Christ, I believe I shall also live with Him.

9. Knowing that Christ being raised from the dead, will never die again; death has no more dominion over Him.

10. For in that He died, He died unto sin once: but in that He lives, He lives unto God.

11. Likewise, I also consider myself to be dead indeed unto sin, but alive unto God through Jesus Christ our Lord.

12. I will not let sin therefore reign in my mortal body, that I should obey it in the lusts thereof.

13. Neither will I yield the members of my body (and faculties) as instruments of wickedness unto sin: but I will yield myself unto God, as one that is alive from the dead, and my bodily members (and faculties) as instruments of righteousness unto God.

14. For sin shall not have dominion over me: for I am not under the law, but under grace.

15. What then, shall I sin because I am not under the law, but under grace? God forbid!

16. Don't I know to whom I yield myself servant to obey, his slave I am to whom I obey; whether of sin unto death, or of obedience unto righteousness?

17. But God be thanked, that though I was slave to sin, I have obeyed from the heart that form of doctrine which was delivered unto me.

18. And having been liberated from sin, I became en-slaved to righteousness.

19. I speak in familiar human terms because of the weakness of my flesh: for as I have yielded my bodily

members (and faculties) servants to moral impurity and to ever-increasing wickedness; so now I yield my bodily members (and faculties) once for all servants to righteousness unto holiness.

20. For when I was slave of sin, I was free from the control of righteousness.

21. What fruit had I then in those things whereof I am now ashamed? For the end of those things is death.

22. But now being liberated from sin, and become servant to God, I have my fruit unto holiness, and the end everlasting life.

23. For the wages of my sin is death; but the gift of God for me is eternal life through Jesus Christ our Lord.

Here's the link to that personalized chapter: Personalized Romans 6

If you want to have victory over any carnal inclination, sinful habit, or sexual addiction, here's how to use this chapter:

Make the effort to memorize it Thoroughly.
Put it on your phone, tablet, laptop, or desktop, or print it and keep it in your pocket.
Pull it out when you are in line at the bank or supermarket store and read it, over and over, until it becomes part of your soul and rests at the bottom of your heart.

Quote it back to God before you fall asleep at night.

Speak to the King in His language. Have true fellowship with Jesus Christ.

This is how God will transform your heart with His Word from the inside out from now on. But such freedom is only achievable when you allow His Holy Spirit to work and cleanse you using all the other tools in this book.

You will develop new life-giving neural pathways as you adopt new habits and disciplines. Once established, they will affect your thought patterns redirecting your life and replacing your old ways and idiosyncrasies.

In other words, as God's Word cleanses the deepest chambers of your heart and reins, new thoughts, ingenuity, and creativity will exude from the innermost parts of your being. Now you can bless others with your spiritual gift.

As stated earlier, recovering the surrendered ground, clearing your conscience, memorizing, and meditating on God's Word are significant parts of the steps to freedom. They lay the foundation for a vibrant walk with God.

Self-Examination

Once again, let's pause and review. The points covered in this chapter are essential. That means you have no choice; they are not optional but mandatory if you want freedom.

These steps build the foundation to replace the devil's strongholds on your soul, which make up your mind or intellect, will, and emotions.

Also, suppose you come to God in sincere humility and genuine repentance. In that case, He will eradicate the root of immorality in your heart and reins.

How did you fall into immorality?

Did it develop into a bad habit, insatiable desire, or a stronghold?

The prayer has three essential components, but they only work if you come to God with sincere humility.

Did you genuinely repent? ___________

Did you ask God to cleanse you with the blood of Jesus? ___________

Did you ask God to take back and recover the surrendered ground? ___________

Do you believe He set you free? ___________

If you are not free, do an attitude check:

Are you willing to bow the knee and humble yourself before God Almighty?

Are you willing to admit and recognize your willful desire to sin?

If you are, do you see immorality as an offense against God and a violation of His command against your soul, body, and others?

If you see lust from God's frame of reference, are you willing to correct a wrong to achieve reconciliation with God?

Notice that none of those mentioned above bullet points demand to engage the emotions. You don't have to feel like it, but you MUST be willing.

Genuine repentance produces peace with God, but not without those four bullet points. If you are willing, Jesus can forgive you, cleanse you with His blood, and uproot the stronghold from your heart and reins.

If now you have a clear understanding and see what's required of you, are you willing to come to God in sincere humility and genuine repentance?

If that's your desire, make the prayer personal and tell it to God, meaning the words with all of your heart.

Assuming all the above are true, you are now ready to start a new and victorious life following the ways of God.

You MUST memorize and meditate on Galatians 2:20. It's your first line of defense against temptation. Can you commit to God and tell Him how you will accomplish this vital step?

Over time, a lustful desire became a bad habit and a stronghold. Then, like the roots of a tree, its cords strengthened and penetrated deep into your heart and reins. Now they are robust neural pathways controlling your thoughts and desires.

Only God has the power to uproot a stronghold. However, only you can replace those pathways with memorization and meditation on His Word.

Romans chapter six will accomplish such a feat and develop your shield of faith. It's not optional but imperative that you memorize and meditate on that chapter. Can you make that vital commitment?

———————

Acknowledge the Sins of Your Forefathers

We began the previous chapter by talking about generational curses and how the parents' sins pass down to their children, affecting the grandkids and subsequent generations.

What do we do if they are enslaved by a stronghold and trapped in their sins?

How do we stop the curse? God's Word gives us the answer and the instructions. So, let's discover what the Creator has to say on the subject.

Our natural tendency is to frown upon the one at fault when things go wrong. However, we are not to blame, accuse, or despise our parents or grandparents for passing down their weaknesses. Instead, we must revert the curse into a blessing.

Carefully read the instructions God gave to the children of Israel regarding the sins of their forefathers. Then, if they confess, acknowledge, and repent, the Lord will restore the blessings promised to their ancestors.

"And those of you who are left shall waste away in their iniquity in your enemies' lands;

Also, in their fathers' iniquities, which are with them, they shall waste away.

⁴⁰ But if they confess their iniquity and the iniquity of their fathers, with their unfaithfulness in which they were unfaithful to Me, and that they also have walked contrary to Me,

⁴¹ and that I also have walked contrary to them and have brought them into the land of their enemies; if their uncircumcised hearts are humbled, and they accept their guilt—

⁴² then I will remember My covenant with Jacob and My covenant with Isaac and My covenant with Abraham I will remember; I will remember the land" (Leviticus 26:39–42).

In keeping with God's Word, the old prophet followed those instructions. And that is what we are to do, instead of pointing the finger. It will set us free from feelings of resentment or accusatory attitudes toward our ancestors.

It renders the curse powerless, establishing the pathway to victory. A new blessing will pass down to the next generation. After suffering the effects of their poor choices and wicked decisions, the man of God pleaded on his nation's behalf:

"We acknowledge, O LORD, our wickedness and the iniquity of our fathers, for we have sinned against You" (Jeremiah 14:20).

When the Riverfront Character Inn and Conference Center opened in Flint, Michigan, on October 13, 2000, the city's mayor experienced a challenging but pleasant surprise. It hit him like a bolt from the blue.

Bill Gothard noticed the black mayor had some reserves inaugurating a place run by predominantly white people. Undoubtedly, the resentments cultivated and kept alive by our society raced through his mind.

At that time, the city of Flint, Michigan, was almost 60 percent African American. But the rest of the state, only 14 percent. It's as if the Lord prepared the landscape, timing, and course of events for what was about to ensue.

So, the inauguration day came, geared up and all set to receive a king. However, the mayor did not seem happy and eager to carry on the celebration.

In a wise appeal, the man of God acknowledged the sins and atrocities committed by the white man against the black. Humbly, Bill said something like,

"Mr. Mayor, I acknowledge and recognize how my ancestors wronged your forefathers. I am deeply sorry. Would you forgive us for enslaving your people?"

After a delayed pause and reflection on the confession and acknowledgment, he took a deep breath and said yes. The result was the willing cooperation of his government, and it opened the door to minister to the city.

Such is God's favor in our lives, His children, when we embrace His Word and follow His ways. Keeping and acting on His commands open the windows of heaven to shower us with His unlimited but dynamic grace.

Self-Examination

Let's pause for a moment once again and look inwardly.

Is there anything I blame my mother, father, or grandparents for?

If so, repent of your sin by following the two-step prayer below.

Lord, I recognize I have sinned by blaming my father or mother, and I am deeply sorry. Please forgive me and cleanse me with the blood of Jesus.

Now, dear God, I will follow Your instructions and personalize Jeremiah 14:20 in my prayer:

"I acknowledge, O LORD, my wickedness and the iniquity of my parents, for we have sinned against You."

Forgive us, oh God, and cleanse us with the blood of Jesus, for we pray in His name, amen.

Let's continue with the next point to keep the newfound purity by guarding our hearts through a one-time event.

Dedicate Your Body to God

Sincere humility and genuine repentance are the heart's attitudes that unlock the pathway to God's mercy and free up His forgiveness.

At salvation, the Holy Spirit touches and causes our innermost beings to awaken to a new life in Christ. Our spirits are then reborn.

Like the spark of light that occurs at conception when the sperm and egg come together, the union of God's Holy Spirit with our human spirit creates new life.

That is 100 percent the work of God. However, the rest of the journey is a joint effort. Therefore, Paul writes to the brethren:

"Dear friends, you always followed my instructions when I was with you. And now that I am away, it is even more important. Work hard to show the results of your salvation, obeying God with deep reverence and fear" (Philippians 2:12 NLT).

One of the ways to grow and develop our sanctification is to dedicate our bodies to the Lord. It's a voluntary and conscious commitment that requires determination, humility, and meekness.

Romans 12:1 says:

"Therefore, I urge you, brothers and sisters, in view of God's mercy, to offer your bodies as a living sacrifice,

holy and pleasing to God -this is your true and proper worship" (NIV).

Such an act is a one-time event, much like a wedding ceremony. But in the same manner, Abraham placed his son Isaac on the altar as a sacrifice to God; He commands us to do the same ONCE!

Other examples of single events (Strong's Greek: 3936 (paristémi).

"Now when the days of her purification according to the law of Moses were completed, they brought Him to Jerusalem to present Him to the Lord" (Luke 2:22).

"For we shall all stand before the judgment seat of Christ" (Romans 14:10).

"For I have betrothed you to one husband, that I may present you as a chaste virgin to Christ" (2 Corinthians 11:2).

If you do this, your body becomes the property of God and, therefore, also holy. After that, with God's grace, you may yield your members to God DAILY, as Romans 6:13 states in my personalized version:

"Neither will I yield the members of my body (and faculties) as instruments of wickedness unto sin. But I will yield myself unto God, as one that is alive from the dead, and my bodily members (and faculties) as instruments of righteousness unto God."

Here's a sample prayer to dedicate your body to the Lord. It's simple and to the point. Again, do not let your mind reason out your spiritual commitments to the Lord, but instead, engage your will despite how you feel:

Dear Father in heaven,
I come to You again in the name of your Son Jesus Christ.
Just like Abraham presented Isaac on the altar,
I now placed my body on Your altar once and for all!
I dedicate my body to You, Oh Lord, as a living sacrifice.
I understand it now belongs to You, and therefore, it's holy.
With the enabling power of Your grace, I will yield my eyes, hands,
And all my bodily members as instruments of right-eousness unto You,
For sin shall not have dominion over me!
In the name of Jesus, amen!

In the chatlines, a few men and women have told me, "I don't feel I'm ready for this kind of commitment." But unfortunately, these are the same people that fall back into immorality and can't figure out what went wrong.

They fail to recognize their stubbornness and self-willed attitude are the reasons they are set in their ways. In other words, they are stiff-necked and unyielding to God's Holy Spirit's promptings to go deeper. Therefore, in time, they will be back to square one.

How about you? Is that how you respond? Or do you want God's victory for your life? If so, prayerfully consider your next move because the enemy already plans to get you. Those demons know how to outsmart you and me and cast a lure before our eyes.

Self-Examination

So far, dedicating one's body to the Lord is the most resisted step in this process. If that's you, please know and understand that the enemy of your soul wants you to keep control.

He wants you to refuse Jesus being a living sacrifice. But, unfortunately, that leaves a crack in the back door to infiltrate your life and get you to fall again.

Also, his most effective weapon is the fear of failure. While that is within the realm of possibility, it's only valid for those who disregard the memorization and meditation on God's Word.

Say no to Satan and overcome your fear by coming forward and talk to one of us. We will pray for the dedication of your body with you and set you free from the schemes of the devil.

Review the following questions:

I am 100 percent clear and understand what it means to dedicate my body to the Lord. Therefore, I choose to die to my sinful nature and yield the control of my body to Jesus Christ. ________

I am not 100 percent clear and do not understand what it means to dedicate my body to the Lord. Therefore, I choose not to dedicate my body to the Lord at this time. _______________________

I fear I will fail. For that reason, I will not make this commitment to God. _______________

I am not ready to release and yield 100 percent control of my life to God. _____________________

To Disarm Satan in Your Life, Come Clean!

Let's continue with the next topic, "To disarm Satan in your life, come clean!" This chapter and the next are so crucial that what you decide to do will determine who keeps the hold on your life.

The wisest man who ever lived wrote in Ecclesiastes 1:9:

"What has been, it is what will be, and what has been done, it is what will be done. So, there is nothing new under the sun" (NASB).

"History merely repeats itself. It has all been done before. Nothing under the sun is truly new" (NLT).

Many wise teachers have proclaimed, "The power of sin is in its secrecy!"

Unarguably, each one of those mentors discovered such truth the hard way. We all fight an unvarying battle. God does not inhabit darkness, nor does He approve it. Therefore, He will not bless you as you hide your sin.

If you come clean, you deprive Satan of his most effective weapon against you to control your life. His dominion is nothing more than a series of make-believe inaccuracies. But when mixed with a little bit of truth, they gain a foothold on your soul.

Persuasively, Satan and his demonic spirits argue,

"What you don't know can't hurt you."

"Once you confess to God, you are done."

"Save the embarrassment; keep it to yourself."
"Don't tip the balance of power over you. It's pointless!"
Here are a few of his "reasonable" deceptions to keep you enslaved if you are married:
If you confess to your wife,

> You will destroy her emotionally.
> You will cause her to have nightmares and break out in cold sweats at night.
> You will make her so bitter that she will get physically sick.
> She will lose all respect for you.
> All she will think of you will be a dirty-minded cheater and unfaithful husband.
> Every time she gets mad, she will throw it in your face.
> She will hate you for the rest of her life.
> She will never trust you again.
> Your wife will not stand your touch, much less to be intimate with you.
> Practically, your marriage will be over.

If you confess to your husband,

> You will destroy his confidence as a man.
> He will be so angry.
> He will explode in violence.
> He will never forgive you.
> That will be his excuse to do the same.
> He will make your life miserable.
> He will kill you.
> He will leave you and file for divorce.

If you are single, the enemy will convince you that you are off the hook, especially if you live by yourself. Even though you are not accountable to a spouse, you must have spiritual authority over yourself.

The best influence and guidance are your parents. If they are not around, seek the counsel and mentoring of your pastor or a mature believer. As a result of humility and confession, you will receive a special favor. It comes from above.

"Therefore, confess your sins to one another, and pray for one another so that you may be healed" (James 5:16 NASB).

The opposite of that long list of reasons happens when we are open and honest before God and human authorities. The following verse encapsulates how the Lord favors us with His enabling and sustaining power.

"God resists the proud but gives grace to the humble" (James 4:6).

Undoubtedly, the news will shock your spouse like a bucket of ice water on a quiet winter night. However, the Lord will favor you with His grace. In His time, healing will take place. Now, put yourself on the receiving end.

Do you want to know the naked truth about your spouse, or would you prefer that they keep you under the spell of ignorance and darkness?

The only way to achieve oneness in marriage is to remove all secrets. Then, the Deceiver leaves.

"He who conceals his transgressions will not prosper, but he who confesses and forsakes them will find compassion" (Proverbs 28:13 NASB).

On the ground of your soul (your mind or intellect, will, and emotions), you may allow Satan to build a stronghold of dirty secrets or let God erect a tower of truth,

BUT NOT BOTH! But unfortunately, the pleasures of sin can dim, blur, and blindfold your spiritual eyesight.

"We demolish arguments and every pretension that sets itself up against the knowledge of God, and we take captive every thought to make it obedient to Christ" (2 Corinthians 10:5 NIV).

Well-crafted deceptions are the building blocks of strongholds.

Once in place, they have the strength and energy to choke out God's truth with our permission as we believe them. Then, again, they enfold the mirror with a hazing mantle to becloud our view. "How did I fall?" we wonder, scratching our heads.

A further benefit of confession is to include the children. "No way," most men respond, and back off reaching down for the pistol. It's one of the most humiliating and embarrassing thoughts, causing a man to shrink and shy away to save face.

It's difficult to humble ourselves and admit our shame before our children. However, when they know we have fallen and they happen to cave in, they will be willing to open up about their temptations and failures.

Sons and daughters are Satan's victims when the parents are in bondage. They are like the eaglets in the nest when the mother eagle is in the trap. The parent bird knows its chicks are helpless, but the dad is often clueless.

However, when freedom breaks in the parent's life, being open and honest with the children at their level and with discretion, they can be set free. Through a simple but striking analogy, the Lord Jesus Christ taught us:

"For who is powerful enough to enter the house of a strong man and plunder his goods? Only someone even stronger—someone who could tie him up and then plunder his house" (Matthew 12:29 NLT).

It's easy to get to the children when the cords of their secret sins entangle either the father or mother. The same happens in single-parent homes. Sooner or later, filth and corruption find their way to the little ones.

A single father told me, "My twelve-year-old daughter is hooked on pornography, and I don't know what to do or how to help her." But unfortunately, he delighted in the same addiction. As a result, he was powerless to unshackle her.

The same demon that trapped the father captured his daughter. He repented in a desperate attempt to rescue and set her free. At the same time, this young man turned his life over to Christ.

God's Holy Spirit and His Word empowered him to save his daughter from the strongholds of lust and moral failure. I wished I could report a victory in his little girl's life, but her father did not follow up with me.

However, his example of sincere humility and genuine repentance before God is the best model to emulate to find freedom. A father who liberates his child is a hero like no other, but only an unchained person can help another.

On the other hand, Moses enlightened and gave fair warning to the children of Israel, *"But if you do not do this, you will certainly sin against the LORD—and be assured that your sin will find you out"* (Numbers 32:23 BSB).

There's no such thing as daddy's dirty little secret regarding strongholds. Clean gloves can hide his grimy and stained hands, but not for long. It's like a time bomb waiting to blast off, flying into pieces, or gas leaking from a rusty old pipe.

Solomon warned: ***"The iniquities of the wicked ensnare him, and he is held fast in the cords of his sin"*** (Proverbs 5:22 ESV).

It's time to disarm Satan in your life by coming clean and allowing God's Holy Spirit to set you free.

Self-Examination

Here's another vital step in your journey to recovery and total freedom. Let's answer the following questions so we can go to the next segment and learn how to confess.

I recognize I have sinned in private. ________________

I now understand I empower Satan in my life by sinning in secret. ________________

I have deceived myself believing I only need to confess to God. ________________

I purpose in my heart to open up to my spouse, parents, or mature believer, and children and confess my dark and sinful secrets. ________________

I now understand to achieve oneness in marriage is to remove all secrets. ________________

I now purpose in my heart to allow God to erect a tower of truth in my soul and to destroy the stronghold of dirty secrets. ________________

How to Confess

In her poem, "Come Clean," Yehuwdiyth Y. Yisrael (Crystal da rock) writes in part:

"Come straight; direct and erect. Come with pure intention and not be mean.

Keep it clean, clear, and without fear. But as you come clean come; declare something meaningful, good, positive and that will bring about peace, joy, love, and cheer and not despair."

How do you that? How do you come clean before your spouse, parents, mature believer, or even your children?

If you agree with the statements…

The power of sin is in its secrecy.

The only way to achieve oneness in marriage is to remove all secrets.

Well-crafted deceptions are the building blocks of strongholds.

If you believe they are based on God's truth, then you are ready to allow the Holy Spirit to set you free.

A man with the courage to expose his darkest secrets can only do it if he believes God's Word and resolves to obey Him. But unfortunately, Satan's arguments rank at the top when it comes to coming clean.

Saving face and keeping our prideful self-image goes against the ways of God. Yet, they conceal and keep out of sight why we live fruitless lives, and our spouses wonder if our prayers will always be in vain.

So, the enemy's lies focus on self-preservation and maintaining an intact reputation. However, contrary to human reasoning, King Solomon reveals a powerful two-part secret of the deep wisdom of God:

"The reward for humility and fear of the LORD is riches and honor and life" (Proverbs 22:4 ESV).

God's grace, favor, and peace meet us and become evident as we faithfully cross over the side of confession. Nonetheless, it's like a painful and complicated childbirth delivery that brings new life and a renewed hope for the future.

Getting ready to come clean, we must prayerfully ask the Lord to orchestrate the timing and opportunity. Then, implore for His wisdom to prepare our words carefully. For example, with sincere humility, we can say:

"Honey, may I speak to you for a moment?"

Then say,

"God has convicted me of sin and led me to repentance. I now realize and recognize I failed God and you, and I want to confess it to you. I fell morally in this area, and I am genuinely sorry. Would you forgive me?"

Don't expect your spouse to jump for joy, and thank you for your courage and honesty. On the contrary, they will be shocked but devastated at worst.

Let their brokenness and pain confirm how much you have hurt Jesus Christ and quench His power in your life.

However long the healing process may take, the Lord will reward it with a stronger bond built on truth rather than deception.

Like heart surgery, the scalpel cuts deep into the core with painful but clean slits. However, the recovery process is likely and predictable.

A young wife from the Middle East came online asking for help. "I'm a happily married housewife, but I fell for my neighbor. He's an attractive young man. I want to stop my sexual relationship with him because I know it's wrong; however, I don't know how."

I walked her through the steps to freedom, but she could not get the courage to confess. Finally, a few weeks later, she returned. The young man threatened to tell her husband if she refused him.

After we repeated the steps, she vowed to God to humbly confess. Then, unexpectedly, her husband forgave her, and as only the Lord can do, He provided a better job for him that required them to move.

She was thrilled to receive mercy and forgiveness that led to freedom and a clear conscience. Then, she saw how God worked in their lives, removing the grip on her soul. The words of the old prophet came alive with a fresh new meaning:

"Great is his faithfulness; his mercies begin afresh each morning" (Lamentations 3:23 NLT).

Undoubtedly, she felt like David as he reflected on his failures, pouring out his heart to the Lord in genuine repentance. He wrote:

"For his anger lasts only a moment, but his favor lasts a lifetime! Weeping may last through the night, but joy comes with the morning" (Psalm 30:5 NLT).

It's time to call on God and come clean before your wife, husband, or other human authority.

Self-Examination

My brethren, it's time to come clean. Just like we have read, we must make a vow to God and move straight ahead to conquer the land. Burn the ships and bridges that connect you to your past.

God's Holy Spirit is ready to rescue and restore your moral life. However, Satan will never agree to release his hold on your life. So, the ball is on your court. Hit it hard against the forces of evil.

To receive God's grace and favor and to experience His peace, I now purpose in my heart to confess to my spouse. _______________

I will not listen to Satan's arguments but honor God and His Word. _______________

I will endure the pain and trust God will heal my spouse's heart. _______________

I will remain humble and allow God to work in my life and marriage without pointing any fingers at my spouse. _______________

Fear and Love God

"God sees me always. When I sleep,
He kindly watches near;
He loves the little child to keep,
Who tries to please Him here.

When I'm alone He sees me too,
Though no one else is by;
And every naughty thing I do,
He sees it from on high.

He sees me, too, when I am rude,
And cry, and fret, and tease;
He loves to see me when I'm good
And try mamma to please.

Then, since He sees me day and night,
And is so kind to me,
I must do always what is right,
His gentle child must be." — "God sees me always" by
H. P. Nichols.

Be aware that the Spirit of God is with you every time you catch your breath in inspiration, and each moment your eyes pause in indignation. He is evaluating the thoughts of your mind and the meditations of your heart.

Therefore, you are constantly and inevitably in the presence of the Lord. But as you recognize and embrace it, how could you make the most of it? First, you must practice not walking alone but with Jesus Christ Himself.

"But if we walk in the light, as he is in the light, we have fellowship with one another, and the blood of Jesus, his Son, purifies us from all sin" (1 John 1:7 NIV).

If you dropped to your knees and came clean, you are out of darkness and have stepped into the light. The angel of the Lord reached deep down the dungeon and released you from the shackles of captivity.

God yearns for your intimate friendship and affection. He grieves when you step out of the fellowship with Him. So, listen with both ears and pay attention to these inspirational but passionate words:

"Or what do you think the Scripture means when it says that the Holy Spirit, whom God has placed within us, watches over us with tender jealousy?" (James 4:5 TLB)

If you have lost the zeal and enthusiasm of your faith and prayers, go back to your first love. Don't let the enemy's craftiness build a cobweb of lies and deceit in your mind, will, and emotions.

Instead, please pick up your shield of faith and dust it off! Then, turn around and humbly see the arms of Jesus welcoming you back. It's the key to the light of His Word. Do not fear the enemy, but God. Practice being in His presence because you are.

Suppose Jesus is NOT the preeminent person in your life but a distant second place holder. Someone who is there to catch you when you fall. In that case, all these tips will be optional and sometimes viewed as unnecessary.

On the other hand, if you love God with all your heart, soul, and innermost being, you will do them by attuning your ear to His voice. Your obedience to the Lord will flow, not out of duty or obligation but out of deep devotion to Jesus.

Ask yourself:

> What is the one thing that I desire the most in my life?
> What is it that keeps me awake at night?
> What do I dream about getting, becoming, or accomplishing?

Imagine this fabulous but exceeding the bounds of reason's idea: The Creator of the universe, God Almighty, wants to be your closest and most intimate friend, guide, and protector. But you have your eyes set on a temporal goal.

If Jesus ranks second or third in your life, don't expect Him to compete with a trinket or the conquest of a short-term daydreamed castle. He is not interested in a crowded corner of your heart.

God has no problem opening the windows of heaven to shower and bless each area of your life. However, falling in love with the blessing and His benefits is the issue. Look at His test and promise:

"The one who has My commandments and keeps them is the one who loves Me; and the one who loves Me will be loved by My Father, and I will love him and will reveal Myself to him" (John 14:21 NASB).

Whatever you are excited about and has your full and undivided attention is what you love.

I've found that the closer I walk with Jesus, the less I worry about this world's shiny objects. But the most crucial thing I discovered is that, after God, I love my wife the most. It has the opposite effect of lust. I went through a near-death experience to catch sight of it.

Here's a familiar but often misunderstood verse:

"He who dwells in the secret place of the Most High Shall abide under the shadow of the Almighty" (Psalm 91:1 NKJV).

The secret place is a spot and realm where no one but God can meet with you. For Daniel, it was the lion's den. For Shadrach, Meshach, and Abednego, it was in the fiery furnace, and for Jonah, it was in the belly of a whale.

Neither one could volunteer to enter that territory to support the other. Therefore, only the Lord qualified to meet them there.

I've had my share of opportunities where, in my immaturity, I rejected God's invitation to enter His presence. But as my faith developed, I got it and had a breakthrough.

Briefly, the market crash of 2008 left me penniless, broken, and shattered to pieces. Then, Jesus invited me into that secret place and refocused my life, giving me a new direction.

My online ministry and books result from that sacred encounter with God's only Son, the Lord Jesus Christ. However, the material losses I experienced will never compare to God's purpose for my life.

Did I need such extreme pressure and crushing defeat in my life? You bet I did! It taught me to fear and love God.

Self-examination

What is the one thing that I desire the most in my life?

____

What is it that keeps me awake at night?

____

What do I dream about getting, becoming, or accomplishing?

____

Where does Jesus rank in my priorities?

____

I now purpose in my heart to love God with all of my soul, heart, and strength. To accomplish that, I will rearrange my priorities and my schedule.

____

Lord, what is preventing me to enter the secret place to meet with you?

____

____

Have a Battle Plan

No soldier or athlete goes out into the field without his proper training or fighting gear. He is prepared and ready to give his best to win the victory. The battle against the lust of the flesh is no different and is not territorial. It will happen where you least expect it.

"Be on guard! Be alert! You do not know when that time will come" (Mark 13:33 NIV).

Inevitably, the temptations and arousal of one's lustful passions will come. Satan is busy figuring out how to make you fall if you are a child of God. He's looking for the opportunity to aim his red laser beam at your heart. The old Apostle tells us:

"Walk in the Spirit, and you shall not fulfill the lust of the flesh" (Galatians 5:16).

The easiest way to allure and tempt you is when you are out of fellowship with the Lord. It is a time when you take small steps to provide for your sensual nature's desires. Innocently, you may reason and respond to a social media post, "Let's see what my friend is up to."

Your guard is down (shield of faith), making you vulnerable to an attractive bait. While you are there, a breathless voice suggests, "Hey, check out who wants to be your friend!" Click! "She's cute, isn't she?"

Your Sword is put away, rendering you defenseless. Since you have already landed on her page, you have no choice but to excuse yourself. You reason, "I will look at her pictures only once and see who she is."

Before you know it, your feet are touching the muddy waters. Her images are enticing and captivating. However, a small voice whispers, "Don't pretend you don't see the red flags." That friendly request wants you to come in and visit with her.

When your conscience awakens and alerts you, call on the Lord, turn around, and repent. Jesus is more than willing and able to rescue you and save you from the lion's sharp teeth and claws. Then after:

Pick up your shield of faith and quote Galatians 2:20 from memory.

It will work if you have meditated on it. That verse is your first line of defense like the loaded .45 Automatic Colt Pistol safely holstered on your hip side. However, if you never paid heed to it, you will slip and fall.

Please re-read the chapter on Generational Curses above, and don't skip it like the suggestion box but pay attention to the instructions. They are the mighty weapons against the enemies of your soul.

With such an arsenal, you can have a battle plan to defeat the enemy at temptation quenching the fiery darts hurled at you. But remember, Satan and his demons won't rest till they entangle you again with thorns of lust and deceit.

Start by quoting Galatians 2:20 to God as you go to sleep. Then, visualize yourself dead to sin on the cross with

Jesus. You're not hanging with the Savior to pay for your sins but to die for your old self.

Like a slow-burning fire, it will turn the dough of the Word into a rich golden-brown bread to feed and sustain your hungry soul. But then, when the assaults face you head-on, you will respond with holy fire.

Self-examination

The Scriptures say,

"Work hard to show the results of your salvation, obeying God with deep reverence and fear" (Philippians 2:12 NLT).

"Be on guard! Be alert! You do not know when that time will come" (Mark 13:33 NIV).

"Walk in the Spirit, and you shall not fulfill the lust of the flesh" (Galatians 5:16).

The next temptation and attack against your emotions, dominating your mind and overpowering your will, are around the corner. To prepare, you MUST exercise M & M, which stands for memorization and meditation.

I will memorize and personalize Galatians 2:20. ________

I will memorize and personalize Romans chapter six. ________

I understand this is the primary way to build and strengthen my shield of faith. ________

I understand that M & M is what the Psalmist meant when he wrote:

"Your word I have treasured and stored in my heart, That I may not sin against You" _________ (Psalm 119:11 AMP).

Accountability

God's Word declares:

"We are his people, and the sheep of his pasture" (Psalm 100:3).

Therefore, we are members of one another who belong in the fold. In a different but more significant way, Paul puts it: *"Now you are the body of Christ and individually members of it"* (1 Corinthians 12:27).

There are no companionless or unneeded members in the church. Nor are there solitary, disconnected, or lone wolves in the body of Christ, except the Judas and Demas among us, but they are not born-again believers.

Without exception, we all must be under authority. Having someone to be accountable works wonders. It's part of fearing God. But, of course, the conflicting thoughts abound when guilt is the supporting evidence against us.

We know the Lord will have us confess to that spouse, parent, pastor, or mature Christ-follower who has our best interest at heart. We know our Heavenly Father will discipline us if we lie to our human authority.

To know that this upcoming Monday, we must account for our decisions and behaviors is a deterrent to keep us in line and out of trouble.

Also, it helps us build valuable habits that foster and strengthens spiritual growth. As a result, our physical eyes brighten, and those who know us notice it. Here's Proverbs 28:13 again in the NASB version:

"One who conceals his wrongdoings will not prosper, but one who confesses and abandons them will find compassion."

Many have described fellowship as two fellows in a ship. It's like being in a rowboat with two sets of oars. One can count on the strength of the other to beat the waves and reach the shore if each drips with sweat paddling.

God's compensation for those who humbly follow His ways is receiving mercy and compassion. After many sweaty sunbaking days, teeth-chattering nights, and enduring years of suffering, David wrote, ***"He restores my soul"*** (Psalm 23:3).

On the contrary, as Elijah ran alone for his life from the wicked Jezebel, he fell into despair and depression. He believed he was the only survivor with no one to rely on. However, God's restoration was in order and soon to come. (See 1 Kings chapter nineteen.)

After his massive moral and spiritual failures, in his old age, Solomon recognizes:

"Two are better than one, because they have a good reward for their labor.

¹⁰ For if they fall, one will lift up his companion. But woe to him who is alone when he falls, for he has no one to help him up" (Ecclesiastes 4:9–10).

Self-examination

In His wisdom, God has placed us under human authority. Therefore, we must give an account of our actions. Let's put a checkmark on the following statements that apply to you:

As a married person, I am accountable to my spouse. ________________

As a single person, I am accountable to my parents or mature believer. ____________

If I don't have anyone, I will ask God and my pastor to provide one. ________________

I will be open and honest to my godly mentor and authority. ____________________

He or she may ask any questions regarding my morality. ________________________

If he or she determines necessary, I will give a weekly account. ________________

Please don't take this advice lightly, ask for help!

The Four-Second Rule and Journaling

There's a fleeting moment that exists for every individual just before they do something truly life-altering. It's that flash of insight and sanity that stalls your heartbeat and blood flow - a quick warning - just before you explode and make a fool of yourself.

Or that incredible brief instant of clarity you have before you floor the gas pedal and run the red light. It's a split second of self-admonishment in which you realize that what you're about to do is wrong, but just as quickly choose to ignore that realization and do it anyway.

It's too fast to catch, too bright to see, utterly gone even before you've blinked and therefore, it does a person absolutely no good at all. And yet, there it is. — Heather Killough-Walden

Researchers tell us that, on average, it takes four seconds for a temptation to capture our hearts. Of course, the visual learner's eyes are the easier target. Nevertheless, with the right bait, all of us bite.

If that's the case, it's a long time to look at the offer and let it work its magic to lure and entice us. The creative and sinister minds to make us fall are always at the cutting edge of innovation. They test to see what works.

Therefore, I allow myself only a split second. But that is when it gets me off guard, not when I'm aware of the tempter's indecent schemes. So, for example, if a sensual magazine is lying in a waiting room, why pick it up?

Like ancient Job making a covenant with his eyes, he made a conscious and deliberate commitment to refrain from his natural tendency to look, spy on, and lust after young and attractive women.

He wrote: ***"I have made a covenant with my eyes; how then could I gaze at a virgin?"*** (Job 31:1 ESV) Similarly, my eyesight is diverted and prohibited from looking back by the time one second has passed.

It took a few times, but I developed the habit that worked for me. However, it's a tug of war. If the enemy never stops coming at us with his flaming missiles, we must persist in the same manner to fight purity.

Here's a question for you from your accountability partner: Have you applied the four-second rule this week, and how?

If you are a visual learner, you can journal your thoughts on paper or on your electronic device. It's a great way to relish and pleasure God's faithfulness. For example, notice what the children of Israel did to record their blessings.

"Then those who feared the LORD spoke with each other, and the LORD listened to what they said. In his presence, a scroll of remembrance was written to record the names of those who feared him and always thought about the honor of his name" (Malachi 3:16 NLT).

Documenting your tips, affirmations, and victories will help you stay on track and serve as a guide to refer to in the future. In time, it will become a priceless treasure. So, like the old hymn says, count your blessings.

If you have such a list of marvelous testimonies, your accountability partner can quickly remind you to read and recount your blessings. ***"The Law of the LORD is perfect, restoring the soul; The testimony of the LORD is sure, making wise the simple"*** (Psalm 19:7 NASB).

And when you feel down or discouraged, God's Holy Spirit will remind you to look back at His works in your life if you have them recorded. The Psalms are David's book of remembrances to ponder, swell on, and reflect on God's testimonies.

I am hard-headed like most men. So, one way God forced me to keep my eyes away from looking was a screeching halt on the highway.

I glanced at a beautiful female image on a billboard sign for about a second. Then, when I returned my eyes to the road, I nearly hit the car in front of me. It felt like the Lord pulled my ear hard.

Let's pause again and consider how to apply this tip to our lives.

Self-examination

I purpose in my heart to stop staring and looking back at a sensual image. _____________

I will ask my accountability partner to work with me in this area. _____________

I will memorize and meditate on Job 31:1: ***"I have made a covenant with my eyes; how then could I gaze at a virgin?"*** (Job 31:1 ESV) _________________

I will be conscious of the four-second rule. _____________

Personal Example

Thank you for sticking with me and reading thus far. Let me share how the fire of lust ignited within my soul and stayed in my heart.

One of the most shocking moments occurred when I was about ten years old. Another boy brought to school the centerfold piece of a **Playboy** magazine carefully concealed within a workbook.

Since I attended an all-male school, they passed the novelty around without objection from any girl. But, no doubt, the lewd image marked all of us for life. Like a shockwave, I remember the electrifying look vividly on my classmates' faces.

It awakened an appetite we did not know we had. Like a hibernating bear lying dormant during winter, its belly is now on fire at the daybreak of spring. I bet most young men had a similar experience.

The airbrushed image returned to haunt me from that point forward because it remained fresh in my memory. Such is pornography's hold; it preys on the mind of its unsuspecting victims—especially a vulnerable and unprotected boy without parental guidance.

Even though the material was not readily available, and stores didn't sell to minors, it was ready to assault me at any time, particularly at night. That boy likely took the two-page image from a magazine found at home.

I never purchased pornographic material. However, as a young man, I could never resist looking at women scantily dressed in media or in real life. But I was not alone. My friends' weaknesses were the same.

It seemed like an external force had control of my eyes by pulling a string anchored and fastened to my soul. Though unseeable and undetected, that intangible hand turned my head without my consent.

The involuntary and spontaneous response satisfied a sexual craving, which produced a moment of self-indulgence. But, again, my lower nature dominated and controlled my dormant spirit.

Whenever my conscience accused me and produced guilt, religiosity would compensate for my sins. I would go to Mass on Sunday morning to counterweight my wicked deeds from the previous week.

When I became a believer at nineteen, I discovered that my new birth in Christ did not set me free. Instead, a new awareness enlightened the window of my soul. Deep down in my innermost being, I knew I was offending God.

It made me conscious of the struggle between my flesh and my spirit. For the first time, I realized we need God's power to overcome it. That inner battle is what Paul writes about in Galatians 5:17:

"For the flesh craves what is contrary to the Spirit, and the Spirit what is contrary to the flesh. They are opposed to each other, so that you do not do what you want" (BSB).

Many years passed before I understood it was a root problem anchored at the bottom of my heart. So, it was until I attended the live seminars and conferences. Then, whenever someone touched on those subjects, I took notes.

Also, I studied the materials published by IBLP written by Dr. Bill Gothard and others that the Lord performed heart surgery. It removed the fully developed seed planted in my soul years earlier.

Now, I have the joy of helping many Christian men and women find freedom as they overcome their lustful inclinations and desires. So many have told me, "I can't believe God set me free. I thought I would die with these struggles."

The Word of God is sufficient and powerful to deliver us. It does not exclude those seeking help with same-sex attraction. On the contrary, the Lord Jesus Christ welcomes all with arms wide open.

The steps outlined in this resource can help anyone find moral freedom and restore his walk with Christ for the rest of his time on earth. But also, it empowers you with the tools to help others.

Self-examination

How bad do you want to overcome lust?

Do you recognize you have offended God, and as a result, you quenched His power in your life?

Then make NOT a commitment but a vow to God. When we make commitments, we are in control. We can stop them anytime, like a contract that makes provision for dissolution.

When we make a vow, it's an unbreakable covenant like the love of Christ for us. Similarly, Jesus wants us to reciprocate with the same resolve.

Command: ***"Make vows to the LORD your God and fulfill them."*** (Psalm 76:11).

Warning: ***"When thou vowest a vow unto God, defer not to pay it; for he hath no pleasure in fools: pay that which thou hast vowed"*** (Ecclesiastes 5:4 KJV).

Example: ***"I will fulfill my vows to the LORD in the presence of all his people"*** (Psalm 116:14 CSB).

Mature believers make vows and keep them. Therefore, I resolve to yield total control to the Lord and how to allow His Holy Spirit to guide, break, and lead me to freedom.

———————————

"When thou vowest a vow unto God, defer not to pay it; for he hath no pleasure in fools: pay that which thou hast vowed" (Ecclesiastes 5:4 KJV).

Prayer to Recover Your Heart and Break the Soul Tie

Soul tie means affixing a link to someone who has a significant impact on your intangible self. Chances that you may have formed a soul tie with someone is when you feel a strong connection with them, one that is honest and all-encompassing.

With this in mind, it is possible to have soul ties with people you aren't romantically involved with. A soul tie can be formed with a close friend, a relative, or even an ex-boyfriend or ex-husband who is no longer in your life even for a long time.

In essence, all these soul connections could result in either a godly or ungodly soul tie, as well as a healthy or unhealthy soul tie. This will all depend on the relationship's commitments, promises, and intentions made. — Renee Allen McCoy, Soul Ties.

God intended marriage to be the inseparable union between a man and a woman. Like oxen, yoked together plowing forward in the ups and downs of life, never alone overloading one side of the harness.

But, like two pieces of wood glued together, they cannot easily come apart but break. When the tear begins, it unravels the silk that holds the most fragile and delicate part of our innermost being into one piece.

As we enter the sacred bond of holy matrimony, exchanging vows before God and witnesses, we give our hearts to each other. Then, the Lord fuses them into ONE for life. Early in the Scriptures, the Lord declares:

"That is why a man leaves his father and mother and is united to his wife, and they become one flesh" (Genesis 2:24 NIV).

However, as fallen humans, we tend to take matters into our hands, yielding to the lures of seduction and temptation, leading to emotional injury. As a result, we discover how fragile, delicate, and vulnerable we are.

Long before marriage, we have given our hearts to someone who will not be our life partner but instead left us broken. Innocently simple-minded, we believed infatuation and physical attraction would keep us under the spell forever.

They are now out of our lives, but the damage and the emotional scars remain. The smell of perfume or cologne and the unique song or place can trigger the pain of shattered dreams and unmet expectations.

Unless Jesus heals and restores us, we will have difficulty adjoining a future spouse. It's hard to bear and burdensome to enter marriage with a backpack full of hurtful memories and a broken heart, especially when the scattered pieces are in someone else's possession.

God designed us for connection and attachment to become one flesh. Nevertheless, the two-part heart cannot be unglued or separated, only torn apart. For such reasons, King Solomon warned his son:

"Guard your heart above all else, for it determines the course of your life" (Proverbs 4:23 NLT).

As I heard the sad story of a young woman, she expressed the torment she was experiencing. Then, like a fool in love, she was the victim of heart fraud. But now, she was engaged and scheduled to wed.

Her new relationship was one blessed by both sets of parents. However, she planned to call off her wedding because she could not wholeheartedly enter marriage being soul-tied to her ex-boyfriend.

Being young and naïve, she couldn't figure out why she felt so guilty. The fact that she gave her heart to someone with a smooth tongue but uncommitted is the puzzling but painful issue. "Why can't I get him out of my mind?" she asked herself.

Her fiancé, a fine and godly man, is someone who deserves an open and honest woman without baggage on her back. He desired not a sinless life partner but one cleansed from her past.

After I explained this concept, she became hopeful and encouraged. A ray of light illuminated her soul, perceiving that Jesus not only saves our spirits but also mends and recovers our broken hearts.

After I led her in prayer, she got excited, overjoyed, and forward-looking to exchange vows wholeheartedly because now she was free. Jesus became her Savior in a new but more personal dimension.

The Lord recovered the missing pieces of her broken heart. Her shattered life was now a thing of the past, and to remain there. "From the bottom of my heart, I thank you! I cannot express how much this means to me," she said.

I responded, "Thank the Lord Jesus Christ! He is the ONE who has liberated you." Indeed, the Lord has the power to rescue us from the results of our disobedience. However, the consequences will remain.

Here's a sample prayer to ask God to break the soul tie and recover your heart. But first, you must recognize your sinful willfulness despite being immature. Then, you must decide to give it to Jesus:

Dear Father in heaven,
I come to you in the name of Jesus, your only Son. Father,
I have sinned by giving my heart to this other person.
Oh God! Break the soul tie I have with this person.
Please, Lord, take it back and keep it safe with You.
I don't have the power to set myself free; only You do, oh Lord!
Recover my heart, oh God, and keep it safe.
I now purpose to give You my heart, oh Jesus!
So that You can keep it until You lead me to give it to someone in marriage, oh Father!
For I pray in the mighty name of Jesus, amen!

Praying Out of Temptation Followed by Visualization

Years ago, my wife and I attended a home school conference and listened to businessman and Christian leader Jim Sammons speak. God transformed him into a thriving and fruitful servant out of the ashes of defeat.

Jim spoke his heart out with lots of wisdom from his personal experience. He gave us the following tips for those having trouble memorizing and quoting scripture as a form of self-defense against temptation.

His explanations and examples are somewhat like these and re-written as I remember and understand them. They are simple and effective because they are the product of dwelling in the presence of God. But I have added my personal touch.

The first tip is to pray out of the snare of temptation before stepping into the net. For example, pray for the attracting object instead of dwelling on the lewd image or staring at the passing person.

If it's a woman, ask the Lord to reach down and touch her heart so she will come to the knowledge of His Son Jesus Christ through conviction of sin and genuine repentance. Ask God to bind Satan in her life and open her spiritual eyes.

Call on God Almighty for His favor and grace. Then, visualize Jesus touching the shoulder of such a person and surprising her with His presence. By the time you finish praying, the temptation is gone.

Here's how to do it:

> Call on God: Dear Lord Jesus, touch this person's heart.
> As you pray, command: Satan, in the name of Jesus, get out of this woman's life!
> Now, Lord, open her spiritual eyes removing the blindfold.
> Convict her of sin and lead her to repentance.

The second, when tempted, visualize Jesus on the cross with His body severely scourged and mutilated because of your willfulness to sin and bent on committing transgressions against God.

See His head crowned with deadly thorns and His sinless blood dripping to the ground. Then, not unlike Peter's experience on the night of Christ's passion, Jesus laser-focuses His eyes on you.

Without any words, Jesus is saying to you, ***"This is my body, which is broken for you."***

As your eyes meet His eyes, flee from temptation, escape from the trap set before you, and consider the price Jesus paid for your sins and how much it cost Him to rescue your body, soul, and spirit.

Let that image dominate and transpose any picture the enemy hurls at your eyes and soul.

Self-examination

I purpose in my heart to pray for the object of temptation in the following manner:

Call on God: Dear Lord Jesus, touch this person's heart.

As you pray, command: Satan, in the name of Jesus, get out of this woman's life!

Now, Lord, open her spiritual eyes removing the blindfold.

Convict her of sin and lead her to repentance.

Close your eyes and picture in your mind Jesus looking at you and saying to you, "This is my body, which is broken for you." ______________________

After reviewing that image, I purpose to flee temptation. ______________

The Rubber-Band Technique

"Tired mothers find that spanking takes less time than reasoning and penetrates sooner to the seat of the memory."
— Will Durant

Early in life, we must experience a swat's sting on the rear to learn obedience, turn from wrongdoing, and curb our thought patterns. But on the contrary, the parent and child lose a valuable opportunity to establish order.

Such painful memory serves us well in developing our character and shaping our behavior. I don't remember the words or the issue, but I know the board of education worked. Quickly, I learned my willfulness against authority called for enduring correction.

The wisest man who ever lived wrote:

"A youngster's heart is filled with foolishness, but physical discipline will drive it far away" (Proverbs 22:15 NLT).
Sooner or later, we grow out of that phase without needing more smacks on the soft rear. At four years old, Eddie, my oldest son, told me, "I know you love me because you spank me." He blew me away.
Unfortunately, many young people never received one. Therefore, they can easily fall into trouble suffering

harsher consequences. Unquestionably, they would have chosen a paddywhack on the hindquarters than getting fired at work.

Many counselors have used this method effectively to overcome weaknesses and replace them with new and productive ones when changing negative behavior. But unfortunately, it's like thwack training for unruly adults.

Dr. Doug Weiss has taught for years the rubber-band technique to break the habits of immorality. Each time you catch yourself yielding to an impure thought, looking at a person or image with lust,

Snap a rubber band on your wrist!

The self-inflicted and throbbing irritation can help you stop the bad habit on its tracks and bring you back in line toward your new chosen path.

If you lack the discipline to memorize and meditate on God's Word, perhaps a burning red mark on your wrist will motivate you to start. Once you see, hear, and feel the sting, it will register in your mind's storehouse.

Also, it can be a revealing checkpoint. It will tell you if you are making any progress. For example, out of nowhere, an intruding thought assaulted your mind, and you let four seconds go by…

SNAP!

"Ouch! I should have quoted Galatians 2:20 immediately to quench the fiery dart and stop the attack from the enemy. Next time, I will be alert and ready." That's how the conversation between your spirit and your mind should go.

It's like a trusted old friend who knows you well and has your best interest at heart. Then without warning, he sets off the sucker-punch button behind your head, saying, "Danger, wake up!"

Like cold water on your face, the painful reminder snaps you back to reality and into the ring to protect yourself against the enemy's blows. ***"Your adversary the devil prowls around like a roaring lion, seeking someone to devour"*** (1 Peter 5:8 ESV).

If you have trouble staying on guard and with your shield of faith in place, this technique can be of assistance to you to forewarn thin ice ahead. It will catch you before you drop down into the arctic waters.

Snap! Turn back and review Romans chapter six again!

Use it as a prayer for victory: "Lord, cause this tool to alert me when I step out of fellowship with You, and I begin to yield to temptation. Please remind me to pick up my shield of faith and stay on guard."

For a professionally designed wristband, check out Craig Perra's "Feed the Right Wolf" at: https://www.the-mindfulhabit.com/_

Self-examination

As an added safety guard and painful reminder, I will use a rubber band to snap me back and warn me there is danger ahead. _________________

Also, I will use it to remind me I am stepping out of fellowship with Jesus and pray:

"Thank you, Lord, for this rubber band and reminding me to get back in fellowship with you. I now pick up my shield of faith and quote to you Galatians 2:20."

A Loud and Desperate Cry: Abba Father!

"When the righteous cry for help, the LORD hears and delivers them out of all their troubles" (Psalm 34:7 ESV).

If you meant the prayer of repentance and rededication, you asked God to cleanse you with the blood of Jesus. Then, you humbly implored Him to recover the surrendered ground from the enemy.

Additionally, if you came clean before your authorities, memorized, meditated on His Word, and practiced the other tips but still struggle today, there's one more critical thing to ask God. But it will force you out of your comfort zone.

As seasoned fishermen, the disciples knew what to do when practicing their trade. The sea of Galilee was their playing field and battleground against the elements, no matter how gusty the winds or tempestuous the waves got.

Their collective years of experience could tell us incredible stories of life and death under the inclement and harshest weather in the open waters. However, nothing prepared them for THE STORM.

"One day, he and his disciples got in a boat. "Let's cross the lake," he said. And off they went. It was smooth sailing, and he fell asleep. But then, a terrific storm came up suddenly on the lake.

> ***Water poured in, and they were about to cap-
> size. Then, finally, they woke Jesus: "Master,
> Master, we're going to drown!"***
>
> ***Getting to his feet, he told the wind, "Silence!"
> and the waves, "Quiet down!" They did it. The lake
> became smooth as glass"*** (Luke 8:22–24 MSG).

Astonished and dumbfounded, each man recognized nothing they could do brought about the stillness only Jesus produced. But, no doubt, Psalm 107 became alive and personal as they hit their wit's end.

Some of you set sail in big ships; you put to sea to do business in faraway ports. Out at sea, you saw GOD in action, saw his breathtaking ways with the ocean:

With a word, he called up the wind—an ocean storm, towering waves! You shot high in the sky; then the bottom dropped out; your hearts were stuck in your throats.

You were spun like a top; you reeled like a drunk; you didn't know which end was up. Then you called out to GOD in your desperate condition; he got you out in the nick of time.

> ***"He quieted the wind down to a whisper, put a
> muzzle on all the big waves. And you were so glad
> when the storm died down, and he led you safely
> back to harbor"*** (Psalm 107:23–30 MSG).

Why would God allow us to face such extreme and impossible circumstances? So that we would recognize how inadequate and incapable we are before God Almighty. It's the cure for prideful and self-centered hearts.

A cry for help requires total and unconditional surrender. It does not originate in the mind but in the depth of our innermost being. Therefore, we call out to God with childlike trust and faith in a loud voice.

Let me ask you.

How bad do you want to overcome lust?

What are you willing to do to find freedom and peace?

What would it take for you to totally surrender to Jesus?

Perhaps this will push you over the fence if you have some reserves or hesitations. Five cents worth of pride can keep you in bondage, but you do not know it until you reach the end of your rope.

In the darkest moment of His earthly life, Jesus cried out, ***"Abba! Father!"*** (Mark 14:36)

And so, we are instructed to do the same. Carefully read how Paul puts together the following verse:

"For you did not receive the spirit of slavery to fall back into fear, but you have received the Spirit of adoption as sons, by whom we cry, 'Abba! Father!'" (Romans 8:15 ESV)

If you have tried everything and are at your wit's end, you have no choice but to cry out to God for help with a loud voice in total surrender. So, when they faced the violently raging storm, the disciples called out to Jesus!

The early church followed the same example: ***"And when they had heard, they raised their voice as one to God"*** (Acts 4:24 ABPE).

Here's a sample cry, not a prayer, but a heartfelt supplication to God with a loud voice:

"Oh, God! Abba Father! Deliver me from lust! Deliver me from immorality! Remove the dirty and defiling hook from my soul! In the name of Jesus! And for your glory! Amen!"

As I was thinking on the subject and working the chatlines last night, a young woman whom I will call Mary Magdalene came through asking for help. It seemed like she had been searching for a while, but no satisfying answer yet.

"I have been in unbearable pain with swollen tonsils for a long time," she said. "Nothing the doctors do bring me comfort or relief. I am so tired of this torture," Mary continued feeling hopeless and discouraged.

"Why does God allow this to happen?" Mary asked in desperation and frustration, expecting to find a long-sought answer. But instead, I listened with empathy and compassion as she poured her heart out.

Poor Mary Magdalene was a victim of sexual abuse, and now she was in physical and emotional pain. Her life had become a living nightmare and her heart a reservoir of hurtful and scarring memories.

In a long conversation, first, Mary turned her life over to Jesus. The vertical connection with God got restored. Then, she learned how to forgive the perpetrator from her heart. As she did it, a ray of hope filled her soul.

I gave her the words to say and asked her to tell them to God out loud. Of course, since our communication is through chat, I never know if the person is doing it. But in Mary's case, she took it seriously to please the Lord.

Immediately upon imploring, she responded, "My pain has gone away!" Indeed, Jesus became real and powerful in her life. At the end of our online conversation, and with much gratitude, she wrote:

"I feel blessed, grateful, and free like a bird that flies high without stress."

Such is His favor and grace and the power of crying out when we come to God in sincere humility and total surrender.

"No reserves. No retreats. No regrets." — William Borden

Self-examination

The most common reason we can't have total victory in overcoming the lust of the flesh is our unwillingness to surrender complete control to Jesus.

Just like the disciples believed they could take the helm and steer clear of the waves, we feel we know how to navigate through the storms of life. However, to show us our lack of total surrender, God orchestrates a circumstantial and overwhelming crisis.

It is then that we need to cry out to God, but are you willing? _________

Can you handle the storm? _________

Are you waiting till lightning strikes? _______

Are you at your wit's ends? _________

Do you still reserve the last word on that matter? _________

Are you willing to release complete control to Jesus? _________

The Final Self-check

"The cruelest thing you can do to someone is force them to hurt alone." — Chris Colfer

"I've been alone my whole life; I can't do it anymore." — James Frey

You cannot make it alone if you are a believer and Christ's follower. An astray dog or a lone wolf can survive in the wilderness, but not a sheep. The predators are more than willing to capture her.

As a member, He placed you within a body. Whether single or married, you are in a community. That implies interaction and relationships with others. Each organ is vital because God's unique gift and design are within each one of us.

If there's baggage from the past, you must take care of it. Any unresolved issue will affect your present and future relationships and how you connect with others, especially a spouse. Then it continues with the children.

For self-reflection, consider the following questions:

Why do you separate and prefer to walk away?
Why do you avoid conflict?
Why do you choose not to participate?

Why do you refuse to work on your personal relationship with your significant other?
Does disagreement or discord trigger a hurtful past?
Have bad past experiences shaped how you think?
What do you fear will happen?
Is what you believe based on a lie?
Are your beliefs based on God's Word?
Why do you escape to pornography or video games?
What do you receive from that escaping activity that you do not get from your spouse?

The enemy of your soul knows that as long as that issue is unresolved, you will never conquer the immoral habit. His lies are reasonable, like, "Everybody has a secret; it's safe within your heart no matter how dark."

Lustful activities will always be there to escape to and offer a false sense of security.

President Ronal Reagan said, "When all fails, tell the truth." That hidden secret will overpower all the tips and words to the wise in this book. If you try them, you will have some success but never total victory and freedom.

It's easier to fade into oblivion or escape to Fantasy Island. However, the longer we stay there, the more we allow the enemy to destroy our greatest assets. Those are our families and relationships.

Satan's lies have the power to keep you in bondage and prevent you from having a fulfilled and meaningful life. If there's a past hurt, his demons will whisper,

"Don't tell anyone what happened to you.

Keep it a secret.

If you bring it out in the open, they will laugh at you."

Anything worth having has a price, risk, and reward. Our calling is not for passivity, skating through life, but to fight for our loved ones and defend the castle, not hide, retreat, or escape out of reality.

"Be on guard. Stand firm in the faith. Be courageous. Be strong. ¹⁴ And do everything with love" (1 Corinthians 16:13–14 NLT).

The excellent and rejuvenating news is that we are not alone and do not rely on our power but on God's Holy Spirit:

"¹⁶ I pray that from his glorious, unlimited resources, he will empower you with inner strength through his Spirit.

¹⁷ Then Christ will make his home in your hearts as you trust in him. Your roots will grow down into God's love and keep you strong.

¹⁸ And may you have the power to understand, as all God's people should, how wide, how long, how high, and how deep his love is.

¹⁹ May you experience the love of Christ, though it is too great to understand fully. Then you will be made complete with all the fullness of life and power that comes from God.

²⁰ Now all glory to God, who is able, through his mighty power at work within us, to accomplish infinitely more than we might ask or think.

²¹ Glory to him in the church and in Christ Jesus through all generations forever and ever! Amen" (Ephesians 3:16–21 NLT).

Self-examination

Just like the coals synergistically produce more fire within the pit, in our spiritual battles, it happens the same.

Separated, we cool off and suffer loss. We are a body in need of one another.

Am I willing to open my heart and stop fighting alone? __________

Do I need help in resolving my present and past issues? __________

Do I believe I am better off apart from the body of Christ? ________

Frequently Asked Questions

"Learn avidly. Question repeatedly what you have learned. Analyze it carefully. Then put what you have learned into practice intelligently." — Edward Cocker

The answers to the following individual questions are not exhaustive but partial and complementary. Many times, there is a multi-layer or reason that keeps a person in bondage. The answer to a related question might be the key.

If we are new creatures at salvation, why do we still struggle with the lust of the flesh?

The day we were born again, God's Holy Spirit touched and united with our spirits to cause the new birth. However, our souls (our minds or intellects, wills, and emotions) remain the same as a field for plowing.

Also, deep in our hearts and reins, there's still a myriad of old habits that embody our character. They are like the members of an old but familiar team. However, now it's our inner enemy and worthy opponent.

Once God saves our spirits, the work of sanctification has just begun. Now our spiritual eyes are open. But a new awareness (our conscience) tells us we are a work in progress. This time we are not alone nor unequipped.

Philippians 2:12 tells us: *"Work hard to show the results of your salvation, obeying God with deep reverence and fear"* (NLT).

James 1:21 shows us how: *"Therefore, ridding yourselves of all moral filth and the evil that is so prevalent, humbly receive the implanted word, which is able to save your souls"* (CSB).

I rededicated my life to Christ but, why do I still fall into sexual sin?

A rededication is an act of the will. However, the passion for good or evil is rooted in the heart and reins (gut). David wrote: *"I delight to do thy will, O my God; thy law is within my bowels"* (Psalm 40:8 JB 2000).

His wisdom and direction are channeled through our reins. *"Behold, thou desirest truth in the inward parts: and in the hidden part thou shalt make me know wisdom"* (Psalm 51:6 KJV).

"Who hath put wisdom in the inward parts? or who hath given understanding to the heart?" (Job 38:36 KJV)

No wonder King David delighted in deep fellowship with God: *"I will bless the LORD, who gives me counsel: my kidneys also instruct me in the night seasons"* (Psalm 16:7 JB 2000).

With such understanding, the shepherd of Israel stated: *"With my whole heart I have sought You"* (Psalm 119:10).

It takes memorization and meditation (M & M) to experience lasting inward change. Also, like a weed, we must unearth the issue with its root from our heart and reins' ground. A rededication means we are willing, and through Christ, we are able.

I attended a deliverance service where they prayed over me, but why can't I conquer this habit?

The power is not in the prayer but in the person of Jesus Christ. He said, *"If you remain in me and my words remain in you, you may ask for anything you want, and it will be granted!"* (John 15:7 NLT)

The Amplified Bible renders the words of Paul written in Colossians 3:16 as follows:

"Let the [spoken] word of Christ have its home within you [dwelling in your heart and mind—permeating every aspect of your being] as you teach [spiritual things] and admonish and train one another with all wisdom, singing psalms and hymns and spiritual songs with thankfulness in your hearts to God."

"Yes, I am the vine; you are the branches. Those who remain in me, and I in them, will produce much fruit. For apart from me you can do nothing" (John 15:5 NLT).

Jesus empowers us to overcome the strongholds of lust as we memorize and meditate on His Word. Not out of duty but out of love for the Savior.

For that to happen, we must come clean before God and our human authorities. In other words, we must be free of any secret lusts. Don't expect the Lord to unshackle you without cutting deep within and experiencing humbling shame.

I have repented many times. So why won't God deliver me from this weakness?

Repentance is the first of many steps in conquering lust and moral defeat. Second, we must claim the blood of Jesus to cleanse us, and third, ask the Lord to recover the surrendered ground.

"They overcame him by the blood of the Lamb" (Revelation 12:11).

"Nor give place to the devil." Or, "Leave no [such] room or foothold for the devil [give no opportunity to him]" (Ephesians 4:27 AMP).

If you live at home with your parents or are married, you must humble yourself and confess to your authority. If you live independently, you need a mature person to look after your spiritual well-being. Keeping the secret is like hiding the enemy in your camp.

"Confess your sins to one another [your false steps, your offenses], and pray for one another, that you may be healed and restored. The heartfelt and persistent prayer of a righteous man (believer) is able to accomplish much [when put into action and made effective by God—it is dynamic and can have tremendous power]" (James 5:16 AMP).

I have prayed and fasted. I have attended men's retreats and joined support groups, but I cannot conquer porn addiction. What am I missing?

Out of all the tips in this book, zoom in on the one you consider unnecessary or unbefitting. Better yet, discover the one you are not willing to do. Perhaps it's too uncomfortable, and you believe it's inconsequential.

List on paper your reasons and justifications and ask God for input. Let the Holy Spirit give you Jesus's point of view and insights. After you finish, run it by your accountability partner and humbly ask for his counsel.

Remember that the power of sin is in its secrecy. That's how demons maintain their strongholds on the souls of God's people. They don't want you to open to your God-given authorities because you will receive the solution.

Also, paradoxically, while shame causes you to feel the loss of your reputation, red-faced, and regret, God uses your humility to favor you with His grace, mercy, and kindness. He does it through the eyes of your human authorities.

My father struggles with lust, and so do I. After I am free, what should I do?

The one thing we must do is turn the curse into a blessing. It's natural to blame and point the finger at our ancestors for our inherited flaws. However, it's quite the opposite of praying and blessing those whose weaknesses have affected us.

Leviticus 26:39–42 gives instructions on what to do and how to do it. So, as we recognize our guilt and willful desire to sin, we tackle the stronghold together with the favor of God even if your mom or dad is dead.

"We acknowledge, O LORD, our wickedness and the iniquity of our fathers, for we have sinned against You" (Jeremiah 14:20).

As you follow those instructions, ask God for the perfect opportunity to come clean before your father. It might encourage him to do the same. Even if nothing happens, the Lord is working in both of you.

Stories abound where God used a child's humility and repentance to break through a father's heart in bondage. He thought his porn addiction was secret and harmless to his marriage and children. However, he was shocked to discover otherwise.

I seduced someone to sin with me. Now that I am free, how can I help that person?

First, you MUST clear your conscience with that person by asking for her forgiveness. Time does not erase guilt, and there's no safety box within your heart to store it. Without pointing any fingers say something like this:

"God has convicted me of sin, and I am sorry. I dragged you down with me, and I hurt you. Would you forgive me?"

Then, share how God set you free, especially the prayer to dedicate your body to the Lord. Don't expect her to embrace your faith on the spot. Be prepared to fight a battle against the enemy and his strongholds.

I am fully committed to my partner. Why is it wrong to be intimate if we love each other?

Sex is God's ultimate wedding gift. It's intended to melt and fuse two hearts for life. But unfortunately, our fallen nature can justify any behavior, especially one vitally needed in our relationships.

God's ways require patience, faith, and endurance to wait for the right timing. Instead, we yield to temptation and take hold of His gift before He wraps it in white satin laces. We render the ceremony and exchange of vows unessential.

If you genuinely love God, you will honor His Word and authority. Of course, it's not easy to trust and obey. But if you do, He will greatly bless your union, family, ministry, and impact on your world through your example.

On the other hand, the way you willfully disobey God in moderation, your children will dishonor Him in exaggeration. Also, their darkened hearts and spiritual ears will be closed to the voice of God's Holy Spirit.

The lustful passions of the heart degenerate as society bents on "progress."

I confessed to God. Why do I have to admit to my wife or parents?

Often, confession to a spouse or parent is rock hard. However, once you come clean, the power of secrecy is broken. The enemy will do all he can to convince and persuade you to the contrary.

Instead of dissolution in the marriage or fracture in the relationship, the Scriptures promise restoration: *"Confess your sins to one another and pray for one another so that you may be healed"* (James 5:16 NASB).

As you act on your faith, humility, and obedience to God, you will experience His kindness and grace through the eyes of the offended party. Hence, also, His favor upon your life. Now, you can build a relationship based on truth.

I confessed to God and my wife. So why do I have to admit to my children?

It's shocking and horrifying to a father to discover his children are attacked and defeated by the enemy in the same areas of his failure. But he never realized the hole in his umbrella opened the door.

However, the willingness to risk embarrassment and shame is well worth knowing that he's rescuing his children's souls and keeping them safe from the enemy's claws because of his actions. They will honor, respect, and thank him forever.

They won't see their father's humility and confession as weak or disgraceful but as responsible, loving, and heroic. Yes, you may feel relieved if swallowed by the earth that night. But at dawn, you wake up as the victor.

On the other hand, saving face and avoiding a stain on your reputation could mean a small crack left open to tempt your children. Then, they will keep it secret when they struggle, give in, and fall.

A father who confesses to his children can say, "Son, if you ever struggle in this area, I will be here for you, and we will get through this together. I will never shame or embarrass you. Instead, I will watch your back and fight for you."

I confessed to God and my family. Do I have to admit to my church?

Organized religion does not benefit from a confession, but the body of Christ does. We are one organism affecting one another and our communities for good or bad. We either thrive in the spirit or wither in the flesh.

Like Achan in the book of Joshua and Ananias and Sapphira in Acts, their decisions and subsequent actions affected the entire congregation. In both cases, it led to cleansing and collective victory.

God's Holy Spirit will lead the church to self-examination and purification when done wisely. The results will be God's mighty works in that congregation's life. But the Lord might want to start with you alone.

God forgave me of my sinful behavior, and I am free now. However, I feel dirty and unqualified to serve Jesus. Is there hope for me?

The devil's lies are one of the most potent and efficient weapons against us that work like a well-oiled machine. Once forgiven, God does not hold us accountable or responsible for those sins. Instead, He dumps them into the depth of the ocean.

However, Satan is an expert accuser and reminds us of our past. He silences believers by running past God's grace and Christ's blood. If he succeeds in keeping us reflecting on our past failures, he renders us ineffective.

On the other hand, God wants to use us to rescue those tangled up in lust and clutched in Satan's grip. If they know Jesus cleanses us with His blood, we can bless them with hope and ignite their faith.

"They overcame him by the blood of the Lamb and by the word of their testimony" (Revelation 12:11).

About the Author

I was born in San Salvador, the capital of the smallest country in Central America, El Salvador. Before my sixteenth birthday, my parents brought my younger siblings and me to Los Angeles, where I started tenth grade.

In high school, I had a classmate who was a drug user and thief, robbed old ladies, and practiced witchcraft. In addition, Enrique possessed an evil power to attract girls and seduce them sexually.

One Monday morning, he appeared different. Not just shaved and clean-cut, but a new brightness replaced the darkness in his eyes. Immediately, I noticed and asked, "What happened to you?"

Instead of his usual wild and crazy partying, Enrique spent the weekend at his uncle's house. They went to church, and there, Enrique heard the gospel. In a nutshell, his response was, "I turned my life over to Jesus Christ."

Over a year, I observed God's transforming power in the life of an evil teenager. I knew his ways and expected Enrique to fall back into drugs and immorality. But instead, his new life impacted mine and pierced through my heart.

Not long after, and still, in my late teens, I followed his example. Finally, I turned my life over to Jesus Christ in 1981. At this time, Minnie and I were newlyweds and committed ourselves the same day.

Fortunately, we had a pastor whose vision extended beyond his eyeglasses. Luis Manuel Aguero befriended me and took me under his wing. He asked me to help him publish a monthly newsletter for the church.

Then, he mentored me to lead the youth group in spiritual activities while Julia, his wife, and other mature women began to work with Minnie in the children's department. But "unfortunately," neither one of us had the chance to warm up pews.

We attended several conferences for the next twenty-five years and learned to search and study the Scriptures. We discovered that God has the answers to life's most complex but challenging issues. He has the power to unshackle and set us free.

The insights in this book are part of the wisdom we have learned to apply to our lives. Also, we have used them to help many in the church who struggled with similar issues. When human knowledge and horse sense fail, God's Word remains.

In 2012 I joined www.groundwire.net, which later acquired www.jesuscares.com and other sites. I serve there as a spiritual coach. So, those who are lost or hurting and looking for hope and encouragement visit us to talk.

Since then, I have chatted with over ten thousand people around the globe struggling with life's issues. It doesn't matter if someone connects from an icy and sunless spot in Siberia or a scorching desert in the Middle East; the human heart is the same.

I don't have all the answers. However, each day is a new challenge to discover what God has to say about the struggles we all face in the journey of life on earth. It's breathtaking to see how His Spirit brings us together.

The contributions of many to my life are the wisdom each has learned from the pages of the Scriptures. That is how God meant discipleship works; an old dog teaches the puppies not to hide the bones in the ground but the heart.

"The wisdom that comes from above leads us to be pure, friendly, gentle, sensible, kind, helpful, genuine, and sincere" (James 3:17 CEV).

Indeed, the closer we get to Jesus, the more we experience His favor.

"The reward for humility and fear of the LORD is riches and honor and life" (Proverbs 22:4 ESV).

Pay It Forward

"Our actions are like ships which we may watch set out to sea, and not know when or with what cargo they will return to port." - Iris Murdoch, ***The Bell***

If Jesus has liberated you from the strongholds of lust and immorality, let Him use you to rescue those trapped in shackles of sexual perversion. Now you have the keys to the dungeon and fuel to light the torch. Lead them out to freedom.

The mental and emotional roadblocks they experience are like the walls of old fortified cities. In turn, they become physically incapable. The chains are as secured as a Hans Wagner safe. But you have the code.

Each time they pull against them, the foot of Goliath rests on the iron fetter's end. You can be their David, armed with the stones only Jesus can provide. You will drive it to hit between the eyes with God's direction and guidance.

"The Spirit of the Lord is upon me because he has anointed me to proclaim good news to the poor. He has sent me to proclaim liberty to the captives and recover sight to the blind, to set at liberty those who are oppressed" (Luke 4:18 ESV).

Jesus wants to do that through you to reach the lost, the hurting, and the oppressed. So, they lie awake at night, longing for a bright light to break through their dark cloud. But they are wondering if dawn will ever bring deliverance.

The evil spirits say, "No way in hell!" But you have proven them dead wrong, and their wicked schemes unfit to prevail against the armor of God. You wear the righteousness of Christ now. So, go and use His keys and light to set them free.